The Six Perfections

The Six Perfections

THE PRACTICE OF THE BODHISATTVAS

Lama Zopa Rinpoche

Compiled and edited by Gordon McDougall

Wisdom Publications
199 Elm Street
Somerville, MA 02144 USA
wisdomexperience.org

Library of Congress Cataloging-in-Publication Data for the hardcover edition is as follows:
Names: Thubten Zopa, Rinpoche, 1945– author. | McDougall, Gordon, 1948– editor.
Title: The six perfections: the practice of the bodhisattvas / Lama Zopa Rinpoche;
    edited by Gordon McDougall.
Description: Somerville, MA: Wisdom Publications, [2020] | Includes bibliographical
    references and index.
Identifiers: LCCN 2019025473 (print) | LCCN 2019025474 (ebook) |
    ISBN 9781614295853 (hardcover) | ISBN 9781614296089 (ebook)
Subjects: LCSH: Paramitas (Buddhism) | Spiritual life—Buddhism.
Classification: LCC BQ4336 .T49 2020 (print) | LCC BQ4336 (ebook) |
    DDC 294.3/444—dc23
LC record available at https://lccn.loc.gov/2019025473
LC ebook record available at https://lccn.loc.gov/2019025474

ISBN 978-1-61429-819-9   ebook ISBN 978-1-61429-608-9

25 24 23 22 21
5 4 3 2 1

Cover and interior design by Gopa & Ted2, Inc. Cover photo by Ven. Roger Kunsang.

Printed on acid-free paper that meets the guidelines for permanence and durability of the Production Guidelines for Book Longevity of the Council on Library Resources.

Printed in the United States of America.

CONTENTS

EDITOR'S PREFACE

THE SIX PERFECTIONS—the activities of the bodhisattva—lay out a route map to enlightenment. Once we have attained the precious mind of bodhichitta and become a bodhisattva, we hone that mind, taking it ever closer to enlightenment by training in the six perfections. These are very advanced practices, each perfection fueled by the wonderful mind of bodhichitta and grounded in the wisdom of realizing emptiness.

But what makes them so precious for us is the absolute relevance they have in our daily lives. Each of the six is a skill we can and need to develop right this moment. I often joke that I have attained the perfection of miserliness and impatience, but, really, within these teachings are the tools to overcome the negative minds we all now have—and to develop their positive counterparts.

Who of us is completely generous or never does an action that harms others? And in this world of smartphones and social media, it seems the whole world is suffering from ADHD, unable to focus for more than a second, twitching from one screen to the next in search of some elusive goal. We all need patience, perseverance, and concentration.

Whenever Lama Zopa Rinpoche teaches on the six perfections, either as a whole or by focusing on one or more, he isn't teaching to the bodhisattvas but to us, and his teaching is wonderful advice that shows us how to redirect our lives, making us more generous, moral, patient, and joyful in doing positive actions. Anybody who has sat in front of Rinpoche knows he embodies bodhichitta and wisdom, and his explanation of these subjects is extraordinary. In compiling this book, I hope I have been able to bring even a fraction of the wisdom he has showered us with for over forty years.

In general, quotes in this book have been taken from published texts such as Shantideva's *A Guide to the Bodhisattva's Way of Life* and have been cited accordingly, but some are Rinpoche's own translations, which I've taken from the transcripts. As Rinpoche very often investigates the words within a verse thoroughly, what I have often ended up with is more a paraphrase of the original quote.

To compile this book, I have used teachings stored in the Lama Yeshe Wisdom Archive that have been lovingly recorded, transcribed, and checked by a vast number of people, all working to preserve the precious words of a great teacher. I would like to thank everybody who contributed to this book: those at LYWA, the audio team that recorded the teachings, and the team at Wisdom Publications, who are an inspiration to work with.

I apologize for any errors found in this book; they are 100 percent mine. May this book be the tool to allow people to develop their positive qualities to the maximum degree in order to help others. May whatever merit gained from the creation of this book be dedicated to peace in this troubled world; to the long life, well-being, and fulfillment of the wishes of all our holy teachers, especially His Holiness the Dalai Lama and Lama Zopa Rinpoche; and to the flourishing of the Foundation for the Preservation of the Mahayana Tradition and of the Dharma throughout the world.

Gordon McDougall
Bath, England

INTRODUCTION:
THE SIX PERFECTIONS

....

THE SANSKRIT for perfection is *paramita*,[1] which literally means "gone beyond." The perfections are the practices of bodhisattvas, holy beings who have completely renounced the self; they have transcended selfish concerns and cherish only others.

Each perfection is perfect, flawless. Each arises from bodhichitta and is supported by the other perfections, including the wisdom of emptiness. Because of that, a bodhisattva generates infinite merit every moment, whether outwardly engaged in working for others or not. A bodhisattva's bodhichitta never stops. Even sleeping, there is no self-cherishing; even in a coma, infinite merit is still created.

The six perfections are as follows:

1. Charity (*dana*)
2. Morality (*shila*)
3. Patience (*kshanti*)
4. Perseverance (*virya*)
5. Concentration (*dhyana*)
6. Wisdom (*prajna*)

The first perfection is the *perfection of charity*. Its nature is the virtuous thought of giving. With that thought we perform the three types of charity: giving material objects, giving fearlessness, and giving the Dharma. These encompass all our actions of body, speech, and mind, such as giving material objects, protecting from fear, and giving the Dharma.

The second perfection is the *perfection of morality*, of which there are three types: refraining from nonvirtue, gathering virtuous deeds, and working for others. The first, refraining from nonvirtue, is abstaining from actions that harm sentient beings. The second, gathering virtuous deeds, means completely giving up the thought of seeking happiness for the self, including seeking self-liberation. The third, working for others, means just that—protecting sentient beings from harm as well as helping them in any way we can.

Then there is the *perfection of patience*. The nature of patience is keeping the mind in virtue whenever we encounter disturbance and harm. (We could endure these with a nonvirtuous mind as well, which is why the distinction is made.) There are three types of patience: not retaliating when harmed, accepting suffering, and having certainty about the Dharma. Accepting suffering means our mind remains calm and undisturbed whenever we receive harm from either sentient beings or nonliving things. Having certainty about the Dharma means always abiding in the wish to continuously practice the Dharma no matter what the circumstance.

The *perfection of perseverance* means being happy to practice virtue—specifically, being happy to practice each of the perfections—and doing work for all sentient beings. This includes virtuous actions of the body and speech, such as doing prostrations and reciting mantras.

With the fifth perfection, *concentration*, through both analytical meditation and single-pointed concentration we constantly reflect on the meaning of the teachings and put them into practice. For instance, when we do a *shamatha*, or calm-abiding meditation, using Guru Shakyamuni Buddha,[2] the Buddha is the object of meditation; if we are meditating on bodhichitta, the mind of enlightenment, when we place our mind single-pointedly on bodhichitta, that is the object of meditation.

The last perfection is the perfection of *wisdom*, of which there are two types. One type realizes the conventional (or all-obscuring) truth,[3] which includes the nature of impermanence or the law of cause and effect. The other type realizes the ultimate truth, the emptiness of all phenomena. Generally, the perfection of wisdom refers to realizing emptiness.

The first five perfections develop the method side of the practice, and the perfection of wisdom develops the wisdom side. One of Lama

Tsongkhapa's two main disciples, Gyaltsap Jé,⁴ explained that both the method and the wisdom sides of the path must be developed using only the unmistaken path.⁵ Following a path that is even slightly flawed will not get us there, no matter how much effort we make. And even if we enter an unmistaken path, unless it is complete we will still be unable to become enlightened. Therefore we should diligently follow the complete and perfect path that allows us to fully develop both method and wisdom. This is all based on correct devotion to a fully qualified Mahayana spiritual teacher, one who has studied the Mahayana scriptures extensively.

At the present time, we are only ever concerned with our own happiness. A bodhisattva, on the other hand, has bodhichitta, the aspiration to release others from suffering and obtain ultimate happiness for them, no matter what difficulties the bodhisattva encounters. Our concerns are completely the opposite of those of a bodhisattva. If we wish to attain bodhichitta and become a bodhisattva, we must train in seeing all sentient beings as our mothers and wish to repay the great kindness they have all shown us. This leads to not just love and compassion arising but also *great* love and *great* compassion; with these, we wish all beings without exception to have happiness and be free from suffering, and we wish to bring this about by ourselves alone. When this state of mind becomes spontaneous, we achieve bodhichitta and can then go on to attain enlightenment.

We can only attain enlightenment when we have achieved each of these perfections; it is the infallible route followed by all buddhas. Attaining each perfection depends on the kindness of all sentient beings. As Nagarjuna asked, if there were no sentient beings, who would be the recipients of our charity? Inanimate objects such as trees or mountains cannot receive our charity; only suffering sentient beings can. Similarly, it would be impossible to practice morality without sentient beings. When we practice morality we refrain from harming others. How could we do that if there were no sentient beings? And without sentient beings who try to harm us, how can we develop our patience? Attaining the perfection of patience definitely depends on all kind mother sentient beings, especially those who wish us harm. Without understanding the suffering of other sentient beings, we could never have the perseverance needed to practice the path untiringly for the vast amount of time it will take. To persevere on the path for many lifetimes, maybe eons, until we attain enlightenment, we need the strong determination that our great compassion brings when we understand how sentient beings are suffering. This would be impossible without the existence of these suffering sentient beings.

All six perfections stem from the great compassion we feel for all sentient beings, which produces bodhichitta. That is the very heart of the path.

1 : CHARITY

....

T HE FIRST of the six perfections is the perfection of charity, or
generosity,[6] which is *dana* in Sanskrit and *jinpa* in Tibetan.

Charity is the thought of giving. If we have money and possessions,
of course we can make one kind of charity by giving to others. However,
even if we are poor, utterly without possessions, living an ascetic life,
we can still practice charity. Charity is the *wish* to give rather than the
actual giving, so it does not depend on having things. It is important to
understand this; the perfection of charity is a mental activity rather than
a physical action, so we can practice it without having anything at all.
We can mentally give to others things such as our body, speech, mind,
good karma, merit collected since beginningless rebirths, and so forth.
For instance, when we practice *tonglen*, the practice of mentally taking
others' suffering and giving them our good qualities, we are offering
charity.[7] When we do the giving visualization, we give all our merits of
the three times—past, present, and future—as well as our own body
and happiness.

The action of giving becomes the perfection of charity when we give
purely and utterly without any delusions such as pride. We can do this
by dedicating any positive action we do and whatever merit we get from
that action, ensuring it is never lost. This is very important when we
practice charity or any of the other perfections. It is very easy to give
something and regret it afterward, or to feel proud of our action of giving. It is especially easy to expect something in return for our generosity.
Such minds weaken the act and stop them from being the *perfection* of
charity.

We can mentally offer everything to all sentient beings, or we can
physically offer a cup of tea to one sentient being. Although both are
actions of charity, we need to make our action of giving as pure as

possible by being very careful that the action is done without the slightest attachment to the object we are giving away. When there is still attachment, it is not really charity; when we give without attachment, that is charity.

The pure practice of charity is one of the principal causes of obtaining a perfect human rebirth; the other main cause is morality. Pabongka Dechen Nyingpo[8] said that practicing just one of these perfections is not enough, we must practice both. And so from our own side, practicing charity is vital. When we practice it well and wisely it has great results.

THE PERFECTION OF CHARITY IS A MENTAL STATE

In the chapter on guarding alertness in *A Guide to the Bodhisattva's Way of Life*, Shantideva makes the distinction between physical charity and the perfection of charity by showing how attaining the perfection of charity does not mean a bodhisattva has given every being everything they need. That would be impossible. He said,

> If the perfection of generosity meant freeing the whole
>   world from poverty, then,
> since there still is poverty in the world today,
> how could it have been that the Perfect Ones of the past
> attained this perfect virtue?
>
> It is said that the perfection of generosity is
> the result of the will to surrender to all living beings
> everything that is yours, including the fruit of such
>   surrender.
> Therefore, this perfection is only a mental act.
>
> Where could I lead all fish and other living beings,
>   so that I could avoid killing them?
> But the moment one acquires a dispassionate thought,
> there is agreement that there is perfection of morality.[9]

The perfection of charity is not a perfection because it has rid the world of beggars and needy people. It is not even the perfection of charity when we have freed ourselves from all miserliness. Arhats have overcome miserliness and yet they are not bodhisattvas practicing the perfection of charity. For bodhisattvas, the perfection of charity is the wish, rather than the actual action, to give whatever any being needs, no matter what that is. It is a state of mind. For bodhisattvas, the wish to give their possessions, wealth, and even their bodies in order to help other beings comes effortlessly.

The perfection of charity does not depend on other sentient beings receiving charity from us, nor does it depend on not having any needy beings left. It depends on destroying clinging to what we each consider as ours, such as our body, speech, and mind, as well as our physical possessions and our merits. It also depends on not being attached to the temporal results of giving. As the number of sentient beings is infinite, when we dedicate our action of charity to all sentient beings with a sincere mind, we create infinite merit and we do unimaginable purification. Every time we do this, we come closer to enlightenment because we are working for all sentient beings without limit.

We have attained the perfection of charity when we can give our body to other beings as easily as giving a cup of water or a few vegetables. (Maybe now if we are very hungry it is difficult to contemplate even giving a few vegetables.) Until we reach that state, we need to endeavor not only to give freely but also to ensure that the action is done purely.

Our Worldly Mind Blocks Giving

Even if we have the wish to practice charity, we still often have many negative attitudes and actions to abandon.[10] First, we might not be aware that the action of giving is a mental one and so we feel frustrated because we don't have physical things we can give others. Even if we know this, we might try to give, but we might not create much good karma because we are clouded by delusions such as regret. These negative minds weaken whatever action of charity we do.

It is very important to not have pride when we practice charity.

Giving with pride makes the merit very weak, like a business that has very little profit. It is also important to avoid having expectations of getting something back from our act of giving, such as material benefit or help. Such expectations mean that although we might physically give something to somebody, we are actually doing it for our own benefit. This is not charity. We are still attached to this life's happiness, which means our motivation is for our own temporal happiness and not for the happiness of the person we are giving to. This stops the action of charity from being pure.

In the same way, giving with the expectation of receiving a good reputation or some praise is not pure giving. We give but we hope that others will see how generous we have been and think that we are so good, how despite our wealth we have so much love and compassion. We want to see our name in the newspapers, and we expect respect and admiration from the poor people we give to. In this way, the act of charity is done for our own worldly happiness and not for others.

Say somebody is starving to death and we give them some food, saving their life. Our main motivation for doing the act, however, might have been to be seen as a wonderful, generous, and compassionate person. If so, the action was about obtaining worldly happiness in this life. Our act of giving has allowed them to survive but is it a virtuous or nonvirtuous act? It might seem as if the action is virtuous because we have helped the other person and given them what they wanted, but that is not so. It is actually a nonvirtuous act because our motivation was not to help them but to have some worldly gain for ourselves. Of course, that doesn't mean that if we see somebody in danger we shouldn't help them because our motivation might be impure!

Unless we always check our motivation, it is very difficult to give to somebody else without the selfish attitude creeping in, wanting something in return for our act of generosity. This is because our self-cherishing mind always only ever wants happiness and comfort for ourselves alone.

Say we usually walk straight past a beggar we see in the street every day. However, one day, because there are many people around, we feel a bit self-conscious not to give anything, so we drop a dollar into their cup. If we give because we don't want others to think we are stingy, that is attachment to reputation, a negative mind. We have wasted that opportunity. On the other hand, to give anything, even a few cents, with a sincere heart not only helps the beggar but also becomes a cause for enlightenment for us. To give with a mind unstained by selfish thought is the pure Dharma practice of charity.

Keeping our mind pure—free from pride, miserliness, and so forth—is very difficult for ordinary people like us. If we could give simply, without all these disturbing thoughts clouding our giving, our generosity would be perfect and attaining another perfect human rebirth would be easy. But this is a struggle for most of us. That is why we must always check our motivation and be diligent in observing our karma.

The villagers of Solu Khumbu, where I was born, have a very good custom to protect themselves and others. Because they are incredibly poor, theft is always a problem. Things are often stolen: cooking pots, money—even potatoes. In many villages the people bury pots of their precious potatoes outside to keep them safe, but thieves can generally guess where the pots are buried, and they dig them up. Also, sometimes people borrow things and don't return them, no matter how much the owner complains and shouts.

In such cases of theft, the villagers often go to a monastery and ask the lama there to say prayers and dedicate the merit of the prayer to the thief, totally offering them that thing. Whether or not this becomes a virtuous act does not depend on the lama but on the mind of the victim. If the person can renounce the stolen object completely and offer it to the thief with compassion, then it is virtuous. The owner needs the object, but the thief also needs it, and so by renouncing it and offering it to the thief with compassion, the dedication becomes a virtuous action.

If somebody stole a hundred dollars from us and we cannot do the practice of dedication—if we cannot take the loss upon ourselves and offer the victory to that sentient being; if we still cling to that hundred dollars—how can we perfect the practice of charity? Even without considering how kind that sentient being has been, how precious they are, we should rejoice that they needed something and now they have it. Like us, they want happiness and do not want suffering—in that way they are completely equal to us—so why can't they have that hundred dollars? If we were to find a hundred dollars, how happy we would be. If we were to find a thousand dollars or a million dollars, we would be so surprised and excited. We would clap our hands with joy. So why can't we do the same thing for this sentient being who has come across a hundred dollars?

INTEGRATING THE OTHER PERFECTIONS INTO THE PERFECTION OF CHARITY

Each perfection depends on the other perfections. When we give with the bodhisattva motivation, with the wish to benefit other sentient beings, we are practicing the *morality of charity*. When we maintain our patience even though people might be ungrateful, we are practicing the *patience of charity*. When we avoid any laziness, such as thinking we can practice charity later, and instead give with continuous, strong energy, we are practicing the *perseverance of charity*. In this way, each perfection includes the others.

Since the perfection of charity—along with the perfections of morality, patience, and so forth—belongs to the merit of virtue, and the perfection of wisdom belongs to the merit of wisdom, giving even a cent to a beggar with the *wisdom of charity*, a deep understanding of emptiness, means that we accumulate both kinds of merit.[11]

It is very good to remember that whatever we give lacks even an atom of true existence, that the giver—ourselves—as well as the action of giving and the recipient are all merely labeled as such by the mind. This is the wisdom aspect of our practice of charity. We thus seal the action of charity with an understanding of emptiness.

A simple way to do this, something that gives the feeling of emptiness, is to not cling to the action. Although nothing exists from its own side, we cling to things because that is how they appear to us and we believe that to be so. Instead, we should look at everything as like a dream—subject, action, and object are all like a dream, without an atom of true existence. When we can do this, we lessen the sense that what appears to us as inherently existing actually does exist in that way.

If we cling to the action of charity as inherently existing, we might accumulate merit because of our positive action but we poison that action with the thought of true existence. In *Seven-Point Mind Training*, Geshe Chekawa[12] advised, "Don't eat poisonous food." In other words, don't let the merit we have accumulated be stained by the wrong conception of true existence.

Lama Tsongkhapa advised that if we have ultimate bodhichitta—the realization of emptiness within the mind of a bodhisattva—any merit we accumulate becomes the cause of enlightenment because we accumulate both types of merit. Without bodhichitta, even though we have the realization of emptiness, practicing charity only becomes the cause of liberation from samsara—not the cause of enlightenment. There is a great difference, like the difference between a handful of dust and the whole earth. By having bodhichitta, the merit has infinite results. Bodhichitta makes a great difference.

To practice charity without incorporating these other five perfections, we risk creating disturbances to the success of our practice. It is like a soldier who puts on some armor but fails to protect the entire body, leaving some spots exposed, risking fatal injury.

THE THREE TYPES OF CHARITY

Many texts list three types of charity:

1. The charity of giving material things
2. The charity of giving fearlessness
3. The charity of giving the Dharma

In the context of taking tantric vows, a fourth type of charity is mentioned, which is the charity of giving loving-kindness.

1. The Charity of Giving Material Things

The first of the three types of charity is giving material things. This charity can be either physical giving or mental giving. The recipient of our giving must be another sentient being, although we can also make offerings to enlightened beings and to the guru, who is the embodiment of all the buddhas.

Like the other perfections, the perfection of charity is mainly to help us develop our bodhichitta—this is a mental training—and so the motivation should be to attain enlightenment. Because as a bodhisattva we have mentally given away all our possessions and have no attachment to anything, we should feel that whatever we offer others is already theirs, that we have just had it on loan. After safeguarding it for them, we are now returning it to its rightful owner.

We should see the receiver of our gift as our guru, helping us to complete the perfection of charity. If the recipient is an enemy, we should give with loving-kindness; if the recipient is suffering and miserable, we should give with compassion; if they are our superior in merit, we should give with rejoicing; if they are equal in merit, we should give with equanimity.

We should also give with joy. Rejoicing is an incredibly important practice, especially for people in the West, who are brought up in a very competitive education system. It seems to me that almost everything in the West—the schooling, the competition for jobs, even sports—is designed to make people strengthen their egos and strive to be better than others. Ambition is seen as a good thing, and somebody who does not try to be better than everybody else is considered weak. This kind of psychological conditioning is the complete opposite of the Dharma mind of thought-transformation practices, which always offers the victory to others.

By giving somebody what they want, we not only make them happy, which should be our motivation for everything we do, but we also come closer to enlightenment; therefore we should rejoice. However, it often happens that when we give, our self-cherishing fools us into feeling we have given away what is ours and what we need in order to be happy, which makes us miserable rather than happy. It can also make us either regret the act or feel proud about it. There are many ways self-cherishing can rob us of our merit.

By giving with the awareness of karma, we can truly rejoice because we see that having created positive karma in the past, we now have the means and the wish to be generous. Furthermore, with this act of giving we create positive karma that will ensure our happiness in the future as well as bring happiness to the recipient of our gift. When we give in this way, we create the habit of giving with joy and it becomes progressively easier. Even if we only do this with a rational mind, one that understands the advantages of giving with joy but without much actual joy in the act, our joy will grow with practice. After we have practiced this way for some time, it will come spontaneously; we will do everything with a Dharma motivation and always feel a deep joy in everything we do.

There Are Many Ways to Practice Charity

We should practice giving in any way we can, unless doing so becomes a hindrance to our Dharma practice. No matter how small it might be, we should use every opportunity to make charity. Take, for example, offering a little blood to a mosquito. Whenever we are hungry, we look for something to eat. The mosquito on our arm is also hungry, and she needs food for her children. She was a human being in previous lives but, not having Dharma wisdom and being under the control of karma, she accumulated the negative karma to be reborn in that insect body. There was no plan. She didn't plan when she was in human form that she would be reborn as a mosquito, in the way that we might study to become a doctor or work to obtain another precious human body.

When we look closely at a mosquito's stomach, it looks completely empty and transparent, a bit like the plastic wrapping that envelops a loaf of bread. The mosquito is starving. By accepting a little pain from her now, we enable her to live and, in return, she gives us enlightenment. That is incredible!

I find thinking like this while remembering the mosquito's incredible kindness is very effective for the mind. Having taken that drop of blood from my arm, she is satisfied and, even though there might be a little pain while she is drinking, I feel real tranquility and happiness watching her fly away. Any pain disappears when I think of her kindness.

There was no wish and no choice at all to be born as a mosquito, a flea, a lobster, or one of those worms that people bait fishing lines with, pushing the hook right through that being's body. They had no choice, and trapped in their animal body, they are so pitiful, utterly without power or guidance. We don't need to think of any of their other sufferings—how they are hungry, thirsty, cold, hot, exploited by humans, and so forth. Just consider how they have taken that body without choice, and because of that, they must experience unimaginable suffering without choice—that is enough.

I often think that feeding birds is an act of charity not only to the birds; by helping the birds rid themselves of hunger, they are less inclined to kill worms for their food. With full stomachs, they sit very contentedly, very peacefully, and so we are feeding the birds and saving the lives of worms.

In Hong Kong and many other places, people help injured or sick animals, forming charities to build animal hospitals where the animals can be treated. We can help animals in many ways. Even if we don't have any money or means to physically give charity, we can make great charity with our mind.

All wealth comes from the wish to give, whereas economic problems such as recessions are caused by the miserly mind. Therefore we should offer physical or mental charity as much as we can. Very often I receive messages from people asking me to help them build monasteries, hospitals, schools, and so forth. Usually I try to help in whatever way I can, but I cannot fulfill everybody's wishes. I try to ensure that people aren't left completely empty-handed—I always offer something—because they are giving me the opportunity to collect merit by practicing charity. Furthermore, if I can give with a bodhichitta motivation, it becomes the cause for enlightenment.

So even if we can't help a person financially this time, and we are not ready to offer our body, there are always ways to practice charity.

Maybe we can't give even a little thing every time but, if we have the means, we should try to give something. That way we help fulfill the other person's wishes and, by creating positive karma, our own wishes will also be fulfilled.

Train Until We Can Offer Our Whole Body

When we are training our mind in charity, we should give without any clinging to the merit of that action. Instead, we should completely dedicate the charitable action so that the being we are giving to is able to find a perfect human rebirth and that we ourselves can reveal the path to them and guide them to enlightenment. If the practice is done in this way, even with tiny actions, gradually our mind becomes stronger and more courageous. Finally, we become like the bodhisattvas, able to give not just a tiny drop of blood to a mosquito but our whole body to a needy sentient being, without any hesitation despite the pain, with only the thought of loving-kindness and compassion.

A favorite story in the *Jataka Tales*[13] is of the time when Shakyamuni Buddha gave his holy body to a family of starving tigers. At that time, Shakyamuni Buddha and Maitreya Buddha were brothers and both bodhisattvas. When they came across a starving tigress and her four cubs in the jungle, they both felt great compassion, but whereas Maitreya left, praying for a fortunate rebirth for the tiger family, the Buddha offered his whole body to them, dying in order to save them from starvation.

The teaching on equalizing and exchanging self and others—one of the two techniques for developing bodhichitta—shows us that all our problems come from cherishing the self and all our happiness comes from cherishing others. Using the practice of tonglen, we learn to renounce the ego, the source of all our problems, and cherish others. With the tonglen practice, when we visualize taking all the suffering of all sentient beings and giving them everything, we are naturally developing the perfection of charity.

For most human beings, the basic problem is the struggle to survive; they lack the means to live. In the practice of giving, we visualize giving them everything they need. For those trapped by poverty, for instance, we visualize billions of dollars falling from the sky like rain for them, until their houses are overflowing with money.

Of course, what they really need is to meet the Dharma and actualize the path, and for that they need to meet a spiritual teacher who can show them the complete unmistaken path to liberation and enlightenment. We can visualize giving them that.

We cannot immediately give everything away to every sentient being and take on the whole suffering of samsara, but we can train with small things. We should develop a strong determination to train our mind until we *can* give them everything and we *can* take the suffering from all beings and experience that by ourselves. With that determination, we do whatever we can according to our capabilities. If we are able to give even a small thing or experience even a small problem on behalf of somebody else, we should do that.

If we cannot even offer a small comfort to another person at present, such as giving a plate of food or a cup of tea, how can we dedicate all our possessions, our body, our happiness, and all our merit collected over the three times to all sentient beings? At present, when we see a free seat on a bus we rush to grab it, and we feel so happy when we beat somebody else to it. Even for such a tiny thing we rush. It's amazing. Yet everybody else on the bus is exactly equal to us in wanting happiness and not wanting suffering; they all want the comfort of that seat as we do.

We all want maximum comfort. I remember a long time ago when I visited a cemetery near Manjushri Institute[14] in northern England, I saw a place where people had reserved their spots to be buried. They were still alive and yet there were pieces of stone with their names on them. Dying is very expensive in the West, and of course it is good to make preparations so that it won't be difficult for other people. But it is pointless to pay for an expensive plot in a beautiful park so the corpse can be comfortable. The person will have died and be utterly unable to enjoy the flowers or the view, and yet they spend so much so their dead body can rot in a beautiful environment. Instead of always insisting on maximum comfort for ourselves alone and spending so much on a piece of land not much bigger than a table, we could use that money in practical ways to benefit others.

We need to start in a small way to train our mind to give progressively more until we can offer everything. In this way, we will gradually be able to offer more, from happily giving up our seat on a bus to bigger and bigger things. Each time we give a scrap of food to a dog or a dollar to a beggar, the thought comes more easily to give more.

Although at this stage our miserliness might stop us from giving anything to anybody, Lama Tsongkhapa explained a technique in which we practice having our right hand offer something to our left hand and vice versa, as if we are giving to somebody else. Of course, we are just giving to ourselves, but still we are practicing giving. To practice giving in this way, the mind is extremely happy and peaceful, which others see and so are made happy. So far, I haven't managed to do this practice.

From there we can start helping others in small ways, such as taking the heavy load from somebody who is struggling. Renouncing our own comfort for others' in that way is exchanging ourselves for others in an extremely small way, but it is a start.

Any practice of offering ourselves to others is based on the understanding that other sentient beings are so precious, so important, so kind. Recalling how they have all been our mothers and kind in four ways[15] will help us see this. By reflecting deeply on the kindness of others, whenever we have dealings with people, that recollection will come spontaneously and the wish to benefit them will naturally be there.

The very fact of our existence, the enjoyments we experience, our ability to follow the path to liberation and enlightenment—all this is due to the kindness of sentient beings. For this reason alone we should renounce the self and cherish others. Because of the kindness of each sentient being, we can accomplish the three great purposes: ensuring the happiness of future lives, attaining liberation, and attaining enlightenment. We should cherish others more than ourselves for the simple reason that this being we call "I" is one, whereas others are countless. No matter how important we might think this I is, it is nothing compared to the importance of the uncountable other sentient beings. Instead of working always for the self, to obtain benefits for ourselves and to prevent our own suffering, we should practice with body, speech, and mind to work for the happiness of others.

2. The Charity of Giving Fearlessness

The second type of charity is the charity of giving fearlessness: guiding others from fear and danger. This can take many forms, such as preventing somebody from endangering themselves or others or giving medicine to protect a person from illness. When a counselor helps a person by advising on what to do and frees them from anxiety, that is also the charity of giving fearlessness.

We also give fearlessness when we show somebody weighed down with worry and fear how to obtain happiness through the Dharma, such as by practicing one of the thought-transformation techniques. When we do that, we are offering not just the charity of giving fearlessness but also the charity of giving the Dharma. When we give the Dharma to others, we protect them from the dangers of this life and from rebirth in the lower realms, so it is naturally the charity of giving fearlessness. Without using Dharma terms, we can show them how to transform problems into happiness and how to benefit all other sentient beings. For somebody with a serious illness, for instance, we can show how it is not just the medication that is important to healing but a good attitude as well.

Kyabje Serkong Rinpoche[16] explained that giving fearlessness includes saving insects that have fallen into water from drowning by lifting them out. If we see animals attacking each other, such as when ants attack a living worm (the dead ones they can have!), we should help if there is a way. Finding some way to keep the ants away from the worm is giving the worm the charity of fearlessness. In the same way, we should save a mouse that our cat has caught. To not intervene, thinking that it is the cat's nature, is not enough. The same logic would mean we do nothing when somebody attacks or abuses us; if somebody tried to kill us, of course we would do everything we could to stop it. We would not simply submit, thinking it was just their nature.

In Solu Khumbu and areas in Tibet, when a person has omens or dreams that suggest they are going to die, or if they have been sick for a long time, it is common for them to consult a lama to receive predictions. One of the recommended common practices is for the person to buy animals such as goats or chickens and keep them in the house, feeding them and caring for them until they die. Sometimes they take the goats to high lamas and ask for prayers or some blessings for them.

If we can also do that, caring for an animal that was destined to be slaughtered, that is very good. By feeding them every day, we perform both the practice of giving material charity and the charity of giving fearlessness, and we create much good karma. In that way, we not only bring happiness to the animal but we also constantly create the cause of our own future happiness.

Animal Liberation Can Incorporate All Six Perfections

According to our own capabilities, we should help protect people and animals from dangers in whatever way we can, trying to guide them from fear. If we are able to protect an animal's life by buying it, rather than allowing it to be slaughtered by a butcher or bought by a restaurant, that is the charity of giving fearlessness. We should liberate animals if we can, depending on how much we can afford. For small creatures, such as fish or worms, we can buy many and do it often. It definitely works. Causing others to have longer lives is itself a karmic cause for our own life to be prolonged by preventing the hindrances that cause untimely death.

With the practice of animal liberation,[17] we buy animals from places where they are going to be killed for food and release them into as safe an environment as possible, somewhere where they can live longer. This can be a simple act or part of an elaborate ceremony involving many people and thousands of animals. In Singapore, Hong Kong, and Taiwan, they don't release animals by the hundreds but by the tens of thousands. So many lives are saved.

It is very beneficial to practice the charity of fearlessness by practically saving their lives while at the same time giving them Dharma imprints by saying mantras and circumambulating stupas or other holy objects with them. The positive potential that they receive from such a practice is unimaginable. On one hand, we are saving their lives, and on the other, we are giving them the causes for full enlightenment. What more can anybody do for such animals?

In this way, such a practice becomes extremely rich. Wishing to save the lives of these kind creatures from the danger of death is the charity of giving fearlessness; feeding them before or after liberating them is material charity; and reciting those powerful mantras and blowing on them, causing them to purify their negative karma and to have good rebirth, is the charity of giving the Dharma.

Besides the perfection of charity, animal liberation contains all the other perfections if we do it correctly. Liberating the animals in this way, we are practicing both the morality of abstaining from nonvirtue and, because we are reciting mantras and circumambulating holy objects with the animals, the morality of gathering virtue. Bearing the hardships of setting up the liberation ceremony and of actually doing it becomes the perfection of patience; the joy and effort we make to do it and the concentration involved become the perfections of perseverance and concentration. And when we see how we ourselves, the animals, and the action of liberating are all nothing other than completely imputed by the mind, the action can become the perfection of wisdom.

Liberating animals in this way is extremely important because if we just buy them from a shop, even when we liberate them there is always the danger they might be killed by other animals. Then what? They can die at any time and most of them will be born again in the lower realms. Of course, there is some benefit in prolonging their lives if we can liberate them where there is no immediate danger from predators, but if we recite mantras and the teachings of the Buddha, such as on emptiness or bodhichitta, it leaves imprints on their minds. Then definitely, after death, they will be in human bodies and able to meet the Dharma, to listen to it, reflect and meditate on it, and actualize the path. That is how they become enlightened. This is what we can offer them; it is something extremely worthwhile.

3. The Charity of Giving the Dharma

While giving things and giving fearlessness are important practices, the most important charity we can give is the charity of giving the Dharma. What sentient beings need is to be free from suffering and its causes and to have peerless happiness, and that can only come when they practice the Dharma. So if we can give them that, what greater benefit can there be?

Giving food, money, or clothing; building schools, hospitals, and so forth—such things are of great benefit to others, relieving them of temporary difficulties, but they are not the greatest benefit. Sentient beings who currently need our material help have all been millionaires in the past countless times, but they are still in samsara; just having wealth alone did not free them from suffering. If it had, all sentient beings would have been freed from suffering an unimaginably long time ago.

What they need is to be liberated from the cause of suffering—not just from sickness, starvation, and the hardships of not having a home. Whereas of course we should give them all the material help we can, we should realize that it alone will not bring more than temporary relief from material suffering. It is not enough. The greatest benefit we can offer others is to lead them from all suffering and to attain the omniscient mind.

Whenever we discuss even a few words of Dharma with somebody with a positive motivation, that is the charity of giving the Dharma. So too are giving teachings, explaining meditations, and reciting mantras and texts. Explaining the Dharma to people is, of course, the best way to truly help people, but if it is done with a bodhichitta motivation, if our reason is to really benefit those people, even gossiping to them—about celebrities, television shows, family business, even sex—is the charity of giving the Dharma. Of course, gossiping is one of the ten nonvirtues and so, in itself, it is negative, but if the motivation behind it is one of loving-kindness and compassion, and if we are doing it in order to generate loving-kindness and compassion in the others' minds, then it is beneficial.

While we recite some Dharma aloud with the motivation that those around us—people, birds, insects, and so forth—hear the holy words and receive the Dharma, we are practicing the charity of giving the Dharma. Even if we are alone in our room, where there are not even fleas, we can still practice Dharma charity by reciting these prayers verbally and visualizing all sentient beings around us receiving our teachings. For instance, because the subject of the *Heart of Wisdom Sutra* is absolute nature, when we recite it we can think at the same time that all sentient beings who have not realized absolute nature before now realize it, that they have understood its meaning.

Say we recite the mantra of the perfection of wisdom: *tayata gate gate paragate parasamgate bodhi soha.* Because it contains the entire essence of the Dharma—the five paths we all must progress through to attain enlightenment[18]—when we recite it in a place where even one being can hear it, even an insect, it plants the seed of enlightenment. Even though that being cannot practice bodhichitta now in this life and enter the path, still in the future it will be able to, because the seed is planted. Either in its next life or after a certain number of eons, it will have the opportunity to hear the teachings and enter into the path because of having heard us chant that mantra even once.

This is how we can help animals. Otherwise, no matter how long they stay with us, no matter how long they live, there is no particular advantage. It makes sense for us human beings who have met the holy Dharma to have a long life, because we then have more opportunity to purify all our obscurations and attain all the realizations and so be best able to help others. We have the practice of refuge, ensuring our life is worthwhile, even if it were to only last another day or a few hours. Animals do not have that opportunity. If they can obtain comfort and decent food, that is the result of previous positive karma, but they are incapable of creating more positive karma and so the positive karma they have is running out. This is like a person who has worked hard and saved a great deal of money but who just squanders it until it is all gone.

Sentient beings suffering in samsara are only liberated through the Dharma. There is no other way to achieve enlightenment; we can't take them there even with the fastest plane, not even by a rocket. When American astronauts landed on the moon and reporters asked His Holiness the Dalai Lama what he thought about it, he explained that while it was the highest accomplishment of science and therefore very good, if it didn't eliminate the three poisons—attachment, hatred, and ignorance—it wouldn't bring peace in the mind. Maybe we should ask those astronauts who landed on the moon whether their three poisons became any smaller.

Make Material Charity Dharma Charity

In Solu Khumbu it was very common for people to offer something to anybody who came to their house. It wasn't that people felt obliged; it was just that they wanted to. Anybody who came to my mother's house would leave with at least some food, despite how poor she was. My father died when I was in my mother's womb, and there was only my sister to help my mother by caring for the animals, until she left to become a nun. Everything else was done by my mother. The rest of us, including me, just played all day.

Whatever my mother got she gave away to others. My brother, Sangyé, earned some money from being a porter on treks, but my mother would give much of it away. She had so much compassion for others. She was always looking after whoever came, especially young monks and nuns. She is an example for us all.

Someone coming to our home is an incredible opportunity to practice charity. When we have a party, we can make it a Dharma party. Our motivation for giving a party is usually for the happiness of this life, to have a good time or to have our friends like us. However, we can transform our party into something worthwhile by changing our attitude. We remember the kindness of our guests, how they have been our mothers in countless previous lives, and then we see the food, drink, and music of the party as offerings to them. In that way the party becomes Dharma. We can make our merit even greater by thinking that all the guests are the embodiments of our guru, such as His Holiness the Dalai Lama, and so whatever we offer to them, we are offering to our guru, which creates great merit.

If some of the people there are disciples of our guru, then we create the most inconceivable merit, even by offering just a glass of water to them. Of course, we can make offerings to a monastery in a faraway place, but making offerings in our own home to somebody who is a disciple of our guru has far greater merit. Not just to the disciples: if the guru is a lay teacher, this includes their partner and children as well as their pets—the guru's horse, dog, cat—as are friends and neighbors. Geshe Chen Ngawa used to send food to his guru's dogs, no matter how far away he was. When people asked him why he did this rather than make offerings to lamas making *pujas* nearby, he explained that offering to the guru's dogs collected far more merit, more merit than offering to the numberless actual living buddhas, the numberless Dharma and Sangha, the numberless statues, stupas, and scriptures.

Adding Dharma charity to material charity is something we should practice as much as we can. For instance, I offer *tsampa* (roasted barley flour) to the ants near my house in Washington, mixing it with water and making it something they can eat. Then, while reciting texts such as the five powerful mantras, I blow on the food to bless it.[19] Adding this Dharma dimension to the way we give to animals, reciting mantras to them and offering them food that has been blessed, can really make a difference to the animals' next lives. As Buddhists we can give our pets this chance that non-Buddhists can't. I think that to have a pet and not do this is a shame.

After I decided to stay in United States and get an American passport—there are so many problems having a Nepalese one—and when the California house was bought, Venerable Roger[20] thought it would be good to have a dog. I thought as Buddhists we should be able to make a difference to the animal's next life, so we named her Om Mani Padme Hum. Having such a name leaves a positive imprint every time she hears her name. We built a stupa at the back of the house for her to circumambulate. The idea was for different people to take her around the stupa every day. There are stories that illustrate how doing this creates the cause for a fortunate rebirth, such as the pig chased around a stupa by a dog that was later reborn in a god realm, or the fly that floated around a stupa on some cow dung that much later, as an eighty-year-old human, attained the arya path. Leading Om Mani Padme Hum around the stupa for half an hour or so a day definitely brought results.

At the Washington house, Buddha Amitabha Pure Land, we had a recording of the *Arya Sanghata Sutra* that I had recorded playing next to the bird feeder day and night. Whenever the birds went there to drink or eat, even if they only heard four words of the sutra, it purified the karma of having committed even the five immediate negativities,[21] saving them from rebirth in the lowest of the hell realms, the inexhaustible hot hell.

As Dharma practitioners, we should see our animals as more than things for our own enjoyment or use, like a farmer might see the cow as nothing more than a source of milk. At Kopan Monastery, I try to say mantras to the cows there—although because they live quite far away behind barbed wire, the chickens that are closer tend to get more mantras. It seems as though the chickens listen. This is in the evening when they are about to sleep and everybody is lined up very nicely on a long pole, looking very cute, like they are going to some meditation or puja. They might have a leader for the puja but they don't tell me.

There was a pigeon who lived on top of Vasubandhu's[22] cave who heard the recitations of the *Treasury of Knowledge*[23] he did every day. After it died, Vasubandhu, through his clairvoyance, found that the being who had been the pigeon was born as a human to a family in the valley below his cave. He asked the family to give him the child, and later on the child became his disciple, the monk called Sthiramati, a great pandit who wrote six volumes of commentaries on the teaching that he had heard when he was a pigeon. As a pigeon the seed was planted, and in the next life he not only became a human being but also did incredible work, having so many realizations and an extensive understanding of the teachings. The cause was insignificant, just hearing the words, but the results were unimaginable.

We should definitely try to make a difference in the lives of our pets and not just look after them by feeding them. We can chant mantras such as those for Maitreya, the Medicine Buddha, or Milarepa, or mantras such as the five great mantras, so that they never get reborn in the lower realms. In that way, having a pet is not just for our own enjoyment but also for the welfare of the animal.

Before we feed our pets, which is material charity, we practice Dharma charity if we chant mantras over the food. Then when they eat the food, not only is their negative karma purified but they also receive the charity of fearlessness. And so offering food—the charity of giving material things—becomes all three charities.

We can recite mantras out loud to animals but also, of course, to people. Even at the beach or places where there are crowds of people, we can chant mantras while we are walking. In Hong Kong once I recited the *Golden Light Sutra* in the street, holding the text and reading loudly so the people passing by could hear. Whatever way we think of that helps becomes Dharma charity.

The Charity of Eating

We can relate the practice of charity to whatever we do in our daily life. For instance, the bodhisattva's yoga of eating is to see ourselves as the servant and all sentient beings as masters, and in order to serve them, to work for them, we eat the food with that attitude. When we eat food in the Mahayana practice, we offer charity to the sentient beings living in our body. This was explained by Nagarjuna in the yoga of eating.[24]

Before we eat, we should offer the food to the beings in our body—the microbes and so forth. Then, in the future, when they become humans, because of the connection made through this act of charity, they will be able to be guided by us revealing the Dharma to them. We should think this way before we eat, that we are bringing them to enlightenment, and then we can really enjoy the food. We can say this prayer:

To the twenty-one thousand creatures living in my body,
I make the charity of this food,
in order that in the future I may
draw them to the Dharma.

I don't know if scientists would agree that there are exactly twenty-one thousand creatures in our body but there are many they have seen with microscopes. Once, in a documentary, I saw food going down the throat and through the body's systems until it came out the other end. All the tiny creatures in our body are so busy, going down and coming up, like cars on a highway.

That's the motivation for eating, to enjoy the food for the sake of all sentient beings, to become enlightened for them. And it's the same thing when we drink something.

2 : MORALITY

WHAT MORALITY IS

THE SECOND PERFECTION is the perfection of morality, which is *shila* in Sanskrit and *tsultrim* in Tibetan. The usual definition of morality is not harming others through actions of body, speech, or mind. In the context of the perfection of morality, however, it is broader than that.

For morality to be a perfection, it should be practiced flawlessly with the other five perfections. Therefore when we give a beggar some food—performing the *charity* of giving material things—that is also the morality of abstaining from harming that being. The *patience* of morality means being patient when others try to harm us and not wishing to retaliate. With the *perseverance* of morality, we continuously keep our morality pure and feel great joy in our positive actions, without following any negative thoughts that might arise. With the *concentration* of morality, we keep the mind single-pointedly on the thought of avoiding nonvirtues by thinking of the benefits of doing so and the shortcomings of not doing so. With the *wisdom* of morality, we keep our Buddhist vows while understanding the emptiness of subject, action, and object—the emptiness of ourselves, the action of not harming, and the one that is not being harmed.

The most effective means to help us maintain our practice of morality is the development of bodhichitta. By constantly thinking on the kindness of other sentient beings and so developing great compassion and special intention, we can easily avoid harming others and come to understand the most skillful ways to benefit them.

The Mind That Cools

The Tibetan word *tsultrim*, meaning "righteous or correct action," refers to keeping pure virtue through mindfulness and awareness, which is also the meaning of the Sanskrit word *shila*, which literally means "cool." When we feel hot and a breeze blows through the house, it cools us down, relieving us of the suffering of being hot. In the same way, samsaric suffering is agitated and hot, and *shila*, morality, is the breeze that cools that suffering.

Whereas the heat of nonvirtue and suffering is created by our negative mind, as Buddhists we have our vows to protect us. By living in the vows, our confusion is overcome and we have no wish to commit actions that are the opposite of morality. While others about us are involved in the worldly affairs that cause them to become agitated and confused and to commit nonvirtues due to desire and so forth, our protecting vows keep us subdued and "cool." Therefore not only do we not harm others when we live in morality but we also protect ourselves from suffering— and, moreover, we purify negative karma we have created in previous lifetimes. In *Hymns of Experience*, Lama Tsongkhapa said,

> Morality is the water that washes off the stains of ill deeds;
> it's the cooling moonlight dispelling the burning agony of
>   afflictions;
> in the midst of people it is most majestic like the Mt Meru;
> it draws together all beings without any display of force.
>
> Knowing this, the sublime ones guard as if they would their eyes,
> the perfect disciplines which they have chosen to adopt.
> I, a yogi, have practiced in this manner;
> you, who aspire for liberation, too should do likewise.[25]

There is a difference between practicing Dharma just because we are scared of the suffering of the lower realms and practicing Dharma because we are trying to receive better future rebirths. Both have value but, like gold is more precious than silver, practicing Dharma with the motivation of attaining a better rebirth is the more precious of the two. By practicing morality we avoid rebirth in the lower realms, but we need to do more than that.

The term *morality* sounds very good, doesn't it? It suggests a very kind heart, something very positive. The description of what morality is—*not* creating any negative actions, *not* harming others—might seem a negation, a *not doing*, but in fact by keeping our vows and overcoming the blocks to better rebirths, liberation, and enlightenment, we are doing the most positive thing we can. The purpose of observing morality is to stop all the hindrances on the path to enlightenment in order to achieve the fully awakened mind. Even so, living a moral life by keeping our vows and not harming others also brings immediate benefits; we naturally feel lighter and happier and less problems come.

There is a huge difference between somebody who is living in morality and somebody who is not. Living in morality is the basis from which all other positive actions can arise. Somebody without the ground of morality will never be able to grow the seed of everlasting happiness and so must not only always suffer but also be unable to avoid harming others. It's that simple.

The Mind That Renounces

Morality is the essential cause of liberation. Avoiding all negative actions of body, speech, and mind, whether through keeping vows we have taken or through living ethically without vows, comes from renouncing worldly concerns.

That does not mean having to live without material possessions or sense pleasures. Many animals live in caves without any possessions, but that is no proof they have minds of renunciation. Near the place where I was born there are a lot of caves that were used by meditators, but these days there are animals there rather than people. When I went there once, the caves were full of yak excrement. If renunciation depended solely on physical separation, then these animals should be renounced beings; they have no possessions at all except their bodies. They eat the grass that is growing nearby and drink the water available, they sleep in caves; they don't talk, they are always in silence. Maybe the animals are great meditators!

If renouncing this life meant physically separating from the things of this life, we would have to separate from our own body. Rather, *renunciation* refers to renouncing the mind that is attached to the worldly affairs of this life, the mind that is attached to this life's comforts. Until we are able to overcome this attachment, it is very difficult to live in morality. Renouncing the worldly mind of attachment is fundamental to leading a moral life. Actual renunciation is the cessation of attachment, anger, and ignorance. As long as we do actions based on these three poisons, we cannot hope for any peace, let alone liberation; they only create more attachment, anger, ignorance, and suffering.

Like charity, morality is a state of mind. Shantideva explained that it is one that wishes to forsake any harm to other beings. If perfecting morality meant protecting all sentient beings from any kind of harm at all, then clearly the buddhas and bodhisattvas have failed because everywhere we look sentient beings are being harmed all the time. However, the incredible wish in the hearts of all the buddhas and bodhisattvas is that no sentient being at all ever receives any harm at all. When we have this constantly and strongly in our own heart we can say we have attained the perfection of morality.

MORALITY IS THE MAIN CAUSE OF A PERFECT HUMAN REBIRTH

The causes for attaining this precious human body are very rare, but without it there is no chance of developing our mind on the path to enlightenment and no chance of escaping the unbearable suffering of samsara. Of this, in *A Guide to the Bodhisattva's Way of Life*, Shantideva said,

> When will I obtain again things so difficult to obtain
> as to be reborn in a world where a Tathagata has appeared,
> as faith in the Dharma, as this human condition,
> as the capacity to practice good,

And, as this peaceful day of today when I am in good health
and I have food to eat?
Life lasts only one instant, it disappoints us.
The body is only like borrowed property.

By conduct such as mine
I will not reach again the human condition.
If I do not attain again human birth, I shall only meet sin,
whence would arise then what is meritorious?[26]

If we cannot make our behavior meaningful now and assure ourselves of another human rebirth, then when we die, which can be at any moment, we will only be reborn in the lower realms and never to know happiness again. Shantideva continued,

If I do not practice good
while I have the capacity to do so,
what shall I do
when the torments of evil destinies blind me?

For he who does not practice
the good and accumulates evil conduct
the word "good destiny" has perished
for hundreds of millions of cosmic ages.[27]

Shantideva showed clearly that if we don't use this opportunity to create the causes to attain another human rebirth, then when we are reborn in the lower realms due to our lack of morality, there is no way we can ever create virtue, trapping us forever in the lower realms.

We must understand that we do not just need an ordinary human rebirth but a perfect human rebirth, one with the eight freedoms and ten richnesses[28] that will give us the opportunity to develop the realizations on the path. The fundamental cause of even an ordinary human rebirth is morality, so how much more so for a perfect human rebirth? First of all, we need to live in pure morality. Then, the causes of the freedoms and richnesses needed to develop on the path are morality and charity combined with a strong longing for such a rebirth.

Developing the other positive qualities allows us to experience the various positive results; for instance, practicing patience causes us to have an environment and people around us that are conducive to our spiritual development. The fundamental cause of this perfect human rebirth is, however, morality with charity as its support. With those two perfections practiced purely and the pure prayer to attain such a rebirth, we can ensure our next life will be totally beneficial.

Morality Is Even More Difficult to Practice Than Charity

It is extremely difficult to find a perfect human rebirth. Just as we are unlikely to own a diamond worth ten million dollars because we simply don't have that amount of money, we are unlikely to have another life like this one because the causes, morality and charity, are so extremely difficult to create.

Practicing charity is very difficult. In the other realms, such as the lower realms or the god realms, practicing charity is impossible. But even in the human realm there are so many internal and external obstacles to our generosity. For morality the obstacles are even greater. When we consider this, we can see the need to keep and maintain Buddhism's various levels of vows.

Generally, practicing morality is more difficult than practicing charity because its essence involves never harming others in any way with any of our three doors of body, speech, and mind. This means having a very deep understanding of karma, an understanding of what results come from what causes.

Although there are billions of human beings on this planet, how many are living in pure morality? This is something we should check for ourselves. The number of people who have taken any of the Buddhist vows is tiny compared to those who have not. We can see this from country to country and from family to family. How many have taken even one vow? The number is very, very small. And if very few people are able to take any of the Buddhist vows, even fewer are able to keep them. To take even one and keep it purely is exceptional. Even in a country such as Nepal that has many Buddhist communities, although everybody would profess to believe in karma, very few actually understand it and even fewer keep pure morality.

Without understanding the difficulty of attaining a higher rebirth, it is hard to see the importance of morality. We might try to meditate but we become lazy, spending most of the meditation distracted. We might earnestly try to keep our vows but become overwhelmed by obstacles that are the disturbances of a deluded mind, creating negative thoughts that lead to negative actions. Like many other people, we might also create nonvirtuous actions in the belief that they are virtuous, based on a flawed understanding of morality.

Disturbances also come from outside, from other living beings. We could be blocked by our family from acting morally, or even by the laws of the country. It is also sometimes difficult to follow morality because, to earn a living, we have to work in a job that harms others in one way or another. We might even feel that by being strictly moral, such as never telling a lie, we might harm somebody. Leading a purely moral life is far from normal in our modern world.

Conversely, just because somebody has taken robes and is supposedly living in the 36 vows, 253 vows, or however many vows there are, that does not necessarily mean that person is living in morality. A monkey can don robes but that does not mean it is following morality.

Morality Is the Basis for the Other Higher Trainings

Liberation from samsara can only happen when we have perfected the three higher trainings of morality, concentration, and wisdom—the wisdom of realizing emptiness. Although we might be able to attain a deep state of concentration without perfecting our morality, this does not constitute a higher training without the other two, and so alone it is not the cause of liberation. For that we need a realization of emptiness, which only comes when insight is conjoined with deep concentration. For that we need pure morality.

In the *lamrim* texts, in the graduated path of the middle capable being, emptiness is not explained, even though it is the fundamental method to be free from suffering. It is only explained in the graduated path of the higher capable being, after finishing the different levels of meditation that lead to bodhichitta. During the middle path, after explaining the suffering of samsara and its causes, karma and delusion, the emphasis is on moral conduct, on keeping the vows.

To have control of our mind in order to use it any way we want, we need concentration, free from distractions and sluggishness. Mostly it is the chattering mind attached to sense objects that arises, distracting us and leading us away from concentration. Only living a moral life can subdue the mind so it becomes like a tamed elephant, one that easily takes the right path, going wherever the trainer wants it to go.

Once, in Drepung Monastery, His Holiness the Dalai Lama explained that to achieve shamatha, or calm abiding—the mind that can stay fixed on an object without distractions—we must have full confidence in our morality. Shamatha can only come through a perfectly calm and clear mind. It cannot be achieved while the mind has any agitation; it cannot come about through taking drugs or alcohol or having some injection. When we achieve shamatha, all other realizations come easily: the renunciation of samsara, bodhichitta, the realization of emptiness, and tantric realizations.

Shamatha has nine levels,[29] but even the first level will not be reached if we have not tamed the mind. If we live in pure morality it is said that we can achieve shamatha very quickly; we may be able to attain the nine levels even within six months. I'm not sure about that; we might need to stop the shamatha practice to do a bit more purification or something like that. Even if we add a few more months—say, a year—to fix whatever mistakes we make, that is still a very short time. It might not even take that long. I heard about a Tibetan lady in Dharamsala who achieved shamatha in two months. On the other hand, I heard of another lady who had been doing a shamatha retreat for many years without success. It depends on how purely the meditator lives in morality.

Because morality is the basis for not only individual liberation but also full enlightenment, we must do our utmost to practice it purely. That means vowing not to harm any sentient being at all in any way. We determine never to kill them, steal from them, lie to them, and so forth. That is the vow; the object is all other sentient beings without exception. Through practicing morality with all sentient beings, through their kindness, we attain all levels of happiness up to full enlightenment.

Actually, we can tell from our own experiences how extremely important moral conduct is. It is very difficult to concentrate when our mind is very disturbed and unclear. With a mind overwhelmed by disturbing thoughts, we cannot meditate at all. Even when we say prayers, we cannot meditate on the meaning of the prayers. Our mind is like a bird swept along by a strong wind, unable to stay still in space for even one moment.

Another analogy is that of clear and dirty water. The mind of a person not living in morality is said to be like agitated water mixed with mud: murky and unclean. In order to see the jewel that is under the water, it is necessary that the water is clean and calm. The mind of a person living in moral conduct is like clean, calm water. The lack of mud is like the purity of the mind and the shamatha is like the calmness of the water. With such conditions, the jewel that lies under the water—the wisdom that realizes emptiness—is easily seen.

In his *Friendly Letter*, Nagarjuna said,

> Keep your vows unbroken, undegraded,
> uncorrupted, and quite free of stain.
> Just as the earth's the base for all that's still or moves,
> on discipline, it's said, is founded all that's good.[30]

Just as the earth is the basis for all moving and unmoving things—all animate things such as animals and inanimate things such as plants—so morality is the basis for all good qualities. It is the root of the Buddhadharma, therefore protecting morality has great benefit, whereas not protecting it has great shortcomings.

Morality is also vital if we wish to practice Vajrayana. Although the tantric path is considered the lightning-quick path to enlightenment, that does not mean, as many of the early Western students of Tibetan Buddhism thought, that tantra can be practiced without a firm foundation of morality, that because Vajrayana seems to be a different path from Sutrayana, which emphasizes morality, morality is unnecessary. That is entirely wrong.

We can understand this when we read the autobiographies of the high lamas of the four traditions who are Vajrayana practitioners, and we see how they maintain such pure morality. We create great negative karma when we think that we don't want to practice the sutra path because it takes so much time, and therefore we give up the discipline of the mind. This is avoiding the Dharma. To feel we are above the moral practices of the Sutrayana is to put ourselves on the path straight to the lower realms.

The Best Practice for Death

Living in morality is not only the best protection in our daily life but also the best preparation for death. With strong morality in our heart, when the time of our death arrives we don't have to rely on others to have a good death. Rather than having regrets or fears as we are dying, we have the great satisfaction of knowing that we have lived a good life and only done positive things, that we have abandoned whatever negative karma we had and lived our life in pure morality.

We have not the slightest fear that we will be reborn in the lower realms. We have complete confidence that we will receive the body of a happy migratory being or, even higher than that, that we will be reborn in a pure land, such as Amitabha's, where there is no suffering at all—no suffering of old age, sickness, death, and so forth—and there is the opportunity to receive teachings from the buddha of that pure land, to practice tantra, and so become enlightened very quickly.

It is mentioned in the teachings that at the time of death the best Dharma practitioner is so happy, as if they are about to go on a picnic or return home to meet their family. A middling practitioner is totally at peace at the time of death; they are unbothered by dying and experience no difficulties. Even for the lower practitioner it is said there are no regrets at the time of death. This is through the power of living in morality.

The Three Types of Morality

In the *Great Treatise on the Stages of the Path to Enlightenment* (*Lamrim Chenmo*),[31] Lama Tsongkhapa explained the three types of morality:

1. The morality of abstaining from nonvirtue
2. The morality of ripening our own mind
3. The morality of working for other sentient beings

The first type of morality, abstaining from nonvirtue, is mainly explained as refraining from creating the ten nonvirtuous actions and developing their opposites, the ten virtuous actions. The second type, ripening our own mind, means doing virtuous actions specifically in order to develop our mind. The third type, working for the welfare of others, means more than just helping other sentient beings with their temporal needs but also leading them into the Dharma so they can develop their own minds toward enlightenment.

The essence of compassion is the wish that all beings be free from suffering, which, from our side, means never harming them; we do this by abandoning all nonvirtuous actions. This is living in morality; it is the very heart of the Buddhadharma. Pabongka Dechen Nyingpo explained that we begin our Dharma practice with protecting our karma, and we begin the path to liberation with the motivation to attain another perfect human rebirth through perfect morality and charity. This is very important. Even if we spend our whole life just watching the breath, unless our practice is possessed by these higher motivations, our meditation simply becomes the cause of another samsara.

With harmful and nonvirtuous thoughts, the wind[32] within our body, which is the vehicle of the mind, also becomes negative. The negative wind then causes the four elements within the body (earth, water, fire, and air) to become unbalanced and disturbed, causing sickness. When sentient beings' four inner elements are disturbed, the four outer elements of earth, water, fire, and air also become unbalanced and violent, resulting in floods, earthquakes, fires, volcanic eruptions, and cyclones, which can destroy whole cities and kill many thousands of people, as well as cause epidemics and famines. Even the planets, the sun, and the moon can become disturbed and harmful.

Living in the discipline of moral conduct, our mind always abides in virtue, imbued with virtuous thoughts, so the four inner elements are balanced and undisturbed, allowing us to remain healthy. This shows that even physical health must come from the mind. Likewise, because the four inner elements are undisturbed, they do not affect the outer elements and cause the external world to become violent and harmful. Without these dangers, sentient beings enjoy happiness.

1. The Morality of Abstaining from Nonvirtue

The first type of morality is the morality of abstaining from nonvirtue. It is what we normally think of as morality—we don't harm others in any way by refraining from committing any of the ten nonvirtuous actions or any other harmful actions of body, speech, and mind. Further, we determine to keep the various levels of vows we have taken.

For us beginners, the three higher trainings are very advanced, something we can only aspire to. But even though shamatha and the wisdom of directly realizing emptiness are beyond us now, we can definitely practice the training of morality by taking and keeping vows such as the *pratimoksha* vows.

It is traditionally said that a country can only thrive when morality is observed by the people of that country. A country with a set of rules based on morality and a system of justice to administer those rules has good crops and people who experience happiness and peace, and the king administering the country attains great renown.

When I went to Tibet, I saw so much negative karma had been created by destroying holy objects such as monasteries and by harming holy beings and other sentient beings. Because of that, the whole place had become very barren and depressed—even the mountains looked depressed! Negative minds and actions affect a country, destroying the richness, the essence, of a place. In the same way, food becomes less nutritional and more difficult to digest, and it very easily becomes the cause of sickness. Even medicines have less power. If there is no discipline in a country, wrongdoers continuously accumulate negative karma and harm themselves and others.

When there is morality, on the other hand, the people and the environment prosper. In the story of the four harmonious brothers, four animals help each other and help the kingdom they live in. The kingdom had been experiencing terrible droughts, famines, fighting, and disharmony, but then, strangely, things changed; rains came at the right time, the crops grew well, and peace and happiness were restored. The king was very pleased and thought it was his leadership that had caused this, but many of the ministers thought that they were responsible. Nobody could agree who caused this newfound prosperity, and everybody wanted to claim responsibility, so the king called in a famous clairvoyant to solve the argument. The sage told the king that the good fortune had been caused by neither him nor the ministers but by four animals living in the forest: an elephant, a monkey, a rabbit, and a pheasant. Not only did they live within the moral discipline of the Buddhist vows, they also showed their disciples how to respect their elders and live with morality. The elephant spread moral discipline among the other elephants, the monkey spread it among the other monkeys, and the rabbit and bird did likewise. This was the cause of the great prosperity of the land. In reality, the pheasant was Guru Shakyamuni Buddha and the three others were his attendants: the elephant was Ananda, the monkey was Maudgalyayana, and the rabbit was Shariputra.

Therefore, even in terms of the benefit to the world, it is very important to put great effort into the very heart of Buddhadharma, into practicing moral conduct and avoiding harming others. There is no question that this is the main practice, the main responsibility, for an ordained person, but even a layperson must try hard to live a moral life and preserve whatever vows they have taken.

Pabongka Dechen Nyingpo said that whether the teachings exist depends on whether the root exists. When he said "root," he was specifically referring to the morality of keeping the pratimoksha vows. If no fully ordained monks or nuns exist, then no matter how many bodhisattvas or tantric practitioners there are, it cannot be said that the teachings exist.

Just as he was about to enter parinirvana,[33] the Buddha was asked by Ananda who could guide them when he was gone. He replied,

> It may be, Ananda, that to some of you the thought may come, "Here we have the words of the teacher who is gone; our Teacher we have with us no more." But Ananda, it should not be considered in that light. What I have taught and laid down, Ananda, as Dharma and Discipline, this will be your teacher when I am gone.[34]

In other words, their guide should be their own morality, based on his teachings on morality and the rules, the Vinaya, he gave to the Sangha. This is all we need to live an ethical life and have peace and harmony in the world.

Avoiding the Ten Nonvirtues by Keeping Our Vows

The fundamental teaching the Buddha gave us for abstaining from non-virtue was to avoid the ten nonvirtues:

1. Killing
2. Stealing
3. Sexual misconduct
4. Lying
5. Harsh words
6. Divisive speech
7. Idle gossip
8. Covetousness
9. Ill will
10. Heresy[35]

Every day we eat, drink, sleep, work, walk, and so forth. Is any one of those actions ever done without attachment to sense pleasure? When we really investigate whether our perfect human rebirth is being wasted or not, we will probably find we have a lot of work to do on our mind. Do we commit any of the ten nonvirtues in the course of a normal day? Do we ever act as if there are no past and future lives or no need for refuge in the Buddha, Dharma, and Sangha?

If we have managed to maintain our moral discipline during even one day, I think that is a cause for great rejoicing. But I think you will find for most of us it is generally far easier to lie, gossip, slander, have ill will, and so forth, than it is to do their opposites. If we could really see the results of our lack of morality, there would be not a moment's laziness. Nothing else would matter; we would only ever think of committing purely virtuous actions.

As Buddhists, we have the perfect way to avoid all nonvirtuous actions and that is by keeping one or more of the sets of Buddhist vows. The foundation, the main practice, is abiding in the five lay vows, the eight Mahayana precepts, or one of the levels of ordination we can take. With the five lay vows, for example, we take the lifetime vow not to kill, steal, commit sexual misconduct, lie, or disturb our mind with intoxicants. With the eight Mahayana precepts, we take the twenty-four-hour vow not to kill; steal; have any sexual contact; lie; eat at inappropriate times (which means after midday); take intoxicants; sit in high seats; or sing, dance, or wear perfume or jewelry.

Even though these are called "general precepts," to receive them is extremely rare. Those keeping the eight Mahayana precepts are rarer than those keeping the five lay vows, and those keeping the thirty-six vows of a novice monk or nun are even rarer. Rarer still are those keeping the vows of a fully ordained sangha. This is because each level of vows is more difficult to keep than the preceding level.

With the pratimoksha vows as the foundation, we need to take and maintain the higher vows, the bodhisattva and tantric vows, to develop our mind toward bodhichitta. The bodhisattva vows are called the treasure of all merits because we take them for the sake of all sentient beings.

Because we take these vows from a guru or preceptor, we need to have already checked the qualities of the guru and seen that they themselves are living in the bodhisattva vows and are learned in the scriptures on bodhichitta and so have the capacity to guide us perfectly. Once taken, we need to protect the vows, never letting them degenerate. We can do that by learning and reflecting on their importance.

The bodhisattva vows are usually given when we receive a tantric initiation and, with a highest yoga tantra initiation, they are given with the tantric vows. There are two levels of the vows we can take: the wishing bodhisattva vow, where we make the sincere wish to attain bodhichitta; and the entering bodhisattva vows, where we promise to refrain from various downfalls. There are eighteen root downfalls and forty-six secondary downfalls. In essence, what we are doing is dedicating our life, as much as we can, to all the kind mother sentient beings.

When we take the bodhisattva vows, we are attempting to totally transform our minds. Sentient beings are numberless. By taking and keeping the bodhisattva vows, we are leading each of these beings out of samsara to full enlightenment. This is something so huge it is unimaginable. If this is not the happiest, most worthwhile thing we can do in our life, then what is?

This is the most important thing we can ever do for all sentient beings, but we have no idea what that means. People talk about world peace, but this world is so small; it is just one tiny world in an infinite number of worlds. When we practice the Dharma, and especially when we follow the Mahayana path with bodhichitta, taking the bodhisattva vows, we are bringing peace to all sentient beings in all universes. The peace of this world comes, by the way, as a side effect. That is how huge our aspiration is.

On top of the bodhisattva vows, we take the tantric vows from a vajra master giving a highest yoga tantra initiation. They are subtler and more difficult to keep, but they are so important. Keeping the bodhisattva vows purely makes it possible to achieve enlightenment, and keeping the tantric vows purely makes it possible to achieve enlightenment quickly.

Unless we pay attention to all these levels of vows, no matter how many mantras we recite, no matter how well we visualize the deity we are practicing, it will have little effect. It will be like painstakingly washing an elephant, only to see it immediately go back to roll in the mud. On the other hand, if we keep our tantric vows purely, even if we don't do any other practice, it is said we can become enlightened in sixteen lifetimes.

Whatever vow we take must be in relation to other sentient beings. We vow not to kill other sentient beings, we vow not to steal from other sentient beings, and so forth. We can only live in morality of the pratimoksha vows because of other sentient beings. Attaining bodhichitta through keeping the bodhisattva vows purely is based on great compassion that sees the suffering of all our kind mother sentient beings. And seeing how unbearable it is that sentient beings are suffering for even a moment, let alone the endless suffering they must endure, inspires us to take and keep the tantric vows purely, to attain enlightenment as quickly as possible to best help them.

The Ten Virtues

Whatever happiness we are experiencing now is the result of positive actions we have done in the past, which means that we lived in the morality of not harming others, such as not killing, stealing, lying, and so forth. Just as there are ten nonvirtues to be avoided, there are ten virtues to be practiced, such as refraining from killing and so forth.[36]

The most amazing happiness we are enjoying is having this precious human body. If we are also enjoying a long life and good health, if we have a comfortable life with enough possessions, then that is due to the kindness of other sentient beings and the morality we have practiced in the past.

When we study the subject of karma, we see there are four kinds of results that occur from our actions. They are the ripening result, the possessed result, the result we experience that is similar to the cause, and the result we create that is similar to the cause. For instance, the ripening result of not killing others in the past is that we attain a precious human body. The possessed result is that we live in a pleasant, conducive environment; living in a place where there is little danger or fear, we can live a comfortable and relaxed life. Furthermore, we experience a long life, which is experiencing the result similar to the cause of allowing others to have a long life, and we can easily refrain from taking life and easily help save lives, which is creating the cause similar to the result. These are four types of happiness we experience from the past positive action of living in the vow not to kill others.

It is similar with the results of the other ten virtuous actions. Living in the morality of not stealing means we again have a precious human body and that we live in a place where we receive rain at the right time, crops are plentiful, and there is no scarcity of food. Having wealth and being free from harm are experiencing the result similar to the cause, and living again in the morality of refraining from stealing is creating the result similar to the cause.

When people don't try to deceive us and when they listen to what we say, that is the result of living in the morality of always telling the truth, of abstaining from lying.

When we are able to live harmoniously with others—our partner or family, work colleagues, friends, other members of our monastery or nunnery—this is due to living in the morality of abstaining from sexual misconduct. Practicing this virtue also results in a beautiful environment, where we live in a very clean place with gardens and flowers. Having perfect surroundings is also the result of not harboring jealous thoughts.

Whenever we hear soothing, pleasing words as opposed to harsh, insulting words, this is the result of ourselves abstaining from using harsh words in the past. When people listen to what we say and believe it, when our words have power, this is through abstaining from gossiping in the past. When we feel peace and contentment, this is the result of not having been covetous in the past, and when we live free from others wishing to harm us, this is because we have lived in the past free from thoughts of ill will.

By understanding karma in this way, we can see how damaging the ten nonvirtuous actions are and how beneficial the ten virtuous actions are. And when we see that all things lack the true existence that we currently think they have, we can then overcome the most harmful nonvirtue: heresy, thinking that nonexistent things exist, and vice versa.

Taking each of the ten virtuous actions like this, we can see that whatever happiness we are experiencing now, have experienced in the past, and will experience in the future is entirely due to having lived in morality. This is true of the mundane happiness we experience in this life as well as the happiness of future lives, the attainment of liberation, and ultimately the attainment of full enlightenment.

2. The Morality of Ripening Our Own Mind

The second type of morality is the morality of ripening our own mind, also called the morality of gathering virtuous deeds. This means doing virtuous actions in order to ripen our mind in bodhichitta, such as listening, reflecting, and meditating on Dharma subjects; making offerings to holy objects; and offering service to the merit field—and, of course, practicing the six perfections.

Any action of abstaining from nonvirtue, the first type of morality, is also a way of ripening our mind, as is working for the benefit of other sentient beings, the third type of morality. And so any action we do from morning until night that is done with the thought to benefit others is ripening our mind—getting up, eating breakfast, going to work, walking, sleeping, and so forth. If it is done with a good heart to benefit others, whether or not it fits into the other two types of morality, we are also ripening our mind in the Dharma.

Whenever we practice charity with a good heart, we are ripening our own mind, and therefore we are practicing this type of morality. Whenever we practice patience, we are ripening our own mind. Whenever we do a daily tantric sadhana,[37] we are ripening our own mind.

Although it can also be called the morality of gathering virtuous deeds, I think the direct translation from the Tibetan, "ripening our own mind," is very meaningful. The Dharma is not harming others and helping them, so whatever Dharma activity we do is naturally a moral action and therefore ripens our own mind, bringing it into virtue.

3. The Morality of Working for Other Sentient Beings

The morality of working for others includes all the virtuous actions we do of body, speech, and mind that are motivated by the thought of benefiting other sentient beings. This includes the four means of drawing disciples to the Dharma[38] and the eleven ways of working for others.

Only when we can refrain from committing negative actions such as the ten nonvirtues can we begin actively working for others.

The Four Means of Drawing Disciples to the Dharma

Whereas the six perfections are means of ripening our own mind, there are four practices that are for ripening others' minds. These are called the *four means of drawing disciples to the Dharma*.

This is the usual translation, but using the term *disciples* makes it a little limited; it actually means drawing all sentient beings to the Dharma—influencing them so we can reveal the Dharma to them and lead them to a better future rebirth and to liberation and enlightenment.

The four means of drawing disciples to the Dharma are these:

1. Giving
2. Speaking kind words
3. Teaching to the level of the student
4. Practicing what you teach

The first means is *giving*, which means giving material things to those who are not yet receptacles for the Dharma. Before we can introduce people to the Dharma, we first make their minds happy by offering what they need materially, such as food and clothes.

The only way to truly help others is through the guidance of revealing the Dharma to them, appropriate to their level of understanding, and to do that, people need to respect us and accept our influence. To simply try to explain the Dharma without having made a connection won't work well; many people just won't listen. By giving material things to those who can be subdued, we develop that connection. In that way, we are bringing them under our influence in order to benefit them.

This is Dharma politics! This is the way Guru Shakyamuni Buddha led sentient beings to enlightenment, and it's the way we ourselves need to lead them to enlightenment. We must reveal the unmistaken path to them in a way that will inspire them to generate the path in their own minds. Only through this can they be liberated completely from all obscurations, develop all the realizations, and so attain the peerless happiness of full enlightenment.

This is how we can skillfully lead them to their greatest wish and give them what they actually need. What has been missing from their lives will be attained. This is so important because there is no other way to free them from suffering. We can't remove their suffering with our hands, like drawing out a thorn or washing them clean with water, and we can't sow the realizations into their minds like planting seeds in a ground.

The second means is *speaking kind words*: that is, talking to people in an appropriate and sweet way—sweet like candy—in a way that pleases them. That is how many of my gurus, such as Geshe Rabten Rinpoche,[39] talked to other people. It was as if he had nothing in his life except chatting with that person, making conversation in a way that was pleasing to the other person just for their pleasure.

Next is *teaching to the level of the student*. That means when we explain the Dharma, we do so in a way that is entirely relevant to the person we are talking to.

The last means is *practicing what we teach*. Just as we explain the Dharma to others, showing them how they can make their lives most meaningful, we too live like that, living in the practice. We exhort them to live in the Dharma, and they can see that we ourselves are doing that—otherwise we cannot be an example for others. Without that inspiration there is no result in the mind, no peace of mind.

The best example of this is Guru Shakyamuni Buddha, who became enlightened countless eons ago, but in order to guide us sentient beings, he appeared in this world system two and a half thousand years ago and showed the twelve deeds: being born, renouncing the worldly life, becoming enlightened, teaching the Dharma, and so forth.[40] In the same way, His Holiness the Dalai Lama has reincarnated for our sakes; he was conceived in his mother's womb, born, grew up in Lhasa, studied with tutors, took ordination, and followed the steps ordinary people must take to achieve realizations. Even though he had no need to do all this, for our sakes he has shown us by example in order to inspire us to study the Dharma and develop our minds on the graduated path to enlightenment.

Like these great teachers, when we have developed our mind, we too will be able to persuade others to live in the practice by setting an example. Even at our current level, we should always try to set a good example for people, even if it is just our immediate family. This is how we can teach others—first our partner and our children, then others. When others see how we benefit from our practice, they can be encouraged to practice too. In that way, we bring peace to our family, neighbors, and colleagues, as well as to the people in our town, our country, and the world. Living our life as much as possible with compassion and setting a good example for others is our best contribution to world peace.

The Eleven Ways of Working for Others

In *Liberation in the Palm of Your Hand*, Pabongka Dechen Nyingpo listed the eleven ways of working for others:

1. Working for those living in poverty
2. Working for those suffering and ignorant of the right method
3. Working to benefit sentient beings who benefit us
4. Working for those threatened with danger and fear
5. Working for those afflicted with miseries
6. Working for the deserted
7. Working for the homeless
8. Working for those without like-minded people
9. Working for those to be able to enter the right path
10. Working for those on the wrong path
11. Working for all through psychic powers[41]

We should do whatever is needed to help sentient beings, such as show-ing the correct road to a traveler who is lost. If we have the capability to help when somebody is suffering or having problems, then we should help them. If that is beyond us at the moment, however, we should work toward being able to have that capability. While we still don't have a buddha's perfect power to guide sentient beings, that goal should be the reason for everything we do.

The first way is *working for those living in poverty*. There are two kinds of poverty: material poverty; and Dharma poverty, which means having no understanding of the Dharma—being ignorant about the four noble truths,[42] karma, and so forth. We should certainly help somebody who is poor in the Dharma.

Living in ordination entails having little desire and being content, and so although a member of the sangha might have very little, they are certainly not poor. The charity they will practice is the charity of giving the Dharma, not giving material things. On the other hand, for those of us not living in ordination, who work for a living and earn a good salary, it is important to help those in need. If somebody is having difficulty finding a place to live, for instance, we should help them find one. Or if somebody is experiencing a disharmonious relationship, we should help them with good advice.

The second way is *working for those suffering and ignorant of the right method*, by trying to help them understand the method. We should try to help them accomplish not only temporal happiness but also what-ever spiritual goal they have; we should definitely help them toward liberation and enlightenment, the ultimate happiness. We should try in whatever way we can to eliminate their ignorance.

We should *work for those sentient beings who benefit us* as a way of repaying their kindness. And we should *work for those threatened with danger or fear*, by trying to rescue them in whatever way we can. If we are able, we should help somebody who is in danger of committing suicide or who is dangerously aggressive or depressed.

We should help those who are possessed by so many worries, which is *working for those afflicted with miseries*. This also includes, of course, *working for the deserted* and *working for the homeless*. If the afflicted person does not want to see us, however, it might not be a good idea, because they will refuse to listen to whatever advice we give; we may even make the situation worse. Of course, how much we are able to benefit and to guide others from suffering depends on how skillful we are.

His Holiness has mentioned this several times. In an interview with a Western sangha many years ago, when he was asked how to explain the Dharma in the West, he replied that because people have various dispositions, it is impossible to say that it should be like this and only offer one explanation. We need to tailor our help depending on the situation and the level of the person we are trying to help.

His Holiness said that even bodhisattvas on the second path, the path of preparation, can only offer ordinary benefit. The ability to offer more than this only comes after reaching the first *bhumi*[43] while on the path of seeing. As we progress through the paths and the bhumis toward enlightenment, the ability to benefit others increases incredibly. There is no comparison possible between the ability of a tenth-bhumi bodhisattva and that of a first-bhumi bodhisattva. However, we should not be discouraged by thinking that if there is that much difference between bodhisattvas at these different levels, then we, who have no realizations at all, are hopeless. With whatever capacity we have now, we should do our best to help others as much as we can, as long as it doesn't harm them instead.

The next way is *working for those without like-minded people*. Without friends and people who share common interests, such as an interest in the Dharma, a person can feel very isolated and unhappy. I know many Dharma students who visit people in hospices and old peoples' homes, really enriching their lives.

Another way is *working for those to be able to enter the right path*. This could have two meanings. The first is helping sentient beings enter the perfect path by explaining the Dharma to them, explaining virtue and nonvirtue, and explaining how to develop the former and avoid the latter. In that way, we can guide them to overcome their delusions and only practice the cause of happiness. The second meaning is to guide them by revealing the infallible right view, the understanding of emptiness, which has the power to completely cut the root of samsara and free them forever from suffering. Then we can guide them on the Vajrayana path without mistakes.

Of course, we should not guide sentient beings at this level if they are not ready. Even if we are able to reveal the very highest teachings, there will be no result, no matter how many eons they dedicate their lives to it. Because of wrong practice and unskillful meditation, instead of reaching enlightenment they could easily get *lung*, wind disease, or become sick or crazy.

Further, we should *work for those on the wrong path*. The previous way is guiding somebody who has not actively entered the wrong path, and so it is easier to show them the unmistaken path. Here, however, because the person has already entered a mistaken path, we must show them how to overcome their difficulties and find the infallible way out of suffering.

Finally, there is *working for all through psychic powers*. This will be beyond us until we attain the state of an arya bodhisattva, when we reach the third path and attain the first bhumi. Then, as our psychic powers develop, we will be able to guide others more and more. For us ordinary sentient beings, however, the best way we can guide other beings is to study the Dharma ourselves and become more skillful in understanding what they need and how to help them get it.

3 : PATIENCE

THE THIRD PERFECTION is the perfection of patience, which is *kshanti* in Sanskrit and *zopa* in Tibetan. My name is Zopa, but that does not mean I am patient. In my case it's just a name, like calling your dog "Buddha."

We all need patience. Even somebody who doesn't practice the Dharma, who doesn't believe in reincarnation, karma, and so forth, needs patience. Otherwise how would anybody have any peace and harmony? How could we possibly get along with our partner, our children, our friends, our colleagues? Even if we were able to find one friend, without patience how could we hold that friendship?

Enlightenment is impossible without patience, and that means we must develop patience for all sentient beings, including those we now think of as our enemies. Enemies are actually the ones we can most learn from—they are, in that way, our best friends and greatest teachers.

In the same way that we need to take the appropriate medicine for an illness we have, we need to practice patience or we will never overcome our anger. Anger destroys our peace, our life; it harms others and turns them against us. A vicious circle begins, causing us to get even angrier. This will continue, even after this life. In a different body we still receive harm from these "enemies" and give them harm in return. For a hundred lifetimes, a thousand lifetimes, this will continue because karma is expandable. Patience is the only antidote.

HOW ANGER ARISES

We begin our training in patience by seeing the real cause of our suffering. The people who have harmed us are not the cause. Controlled by delusion and karma, they were forced to do the actions that harmed us.

When we understand karma, we can see that it is impossible to receive the result of something if we have not created the cause in the past, so we must have harmed that person in some way previously to cause this situation to arise. We have abused them, and now the karma has returned and we are being abused. Whatever negative thing is happening to us at this moment can always be traced back to a similar negative action we did in the past. When we develop a deep understanding of karma, when we have complete conviction that those who harm us could not help harming us because of the previous harm we did them, they become only objects of compassion. We harmed them, and now we are being paid back. We caused this, so how can we possibly become angry with them?

Until we have totally eradicated anger from our mindstream and have a mind of perfect patience, we can still become angry. Somebody could angrily criticize a buddha or even destroy texts and stupas in front of them, but a buddha could never become angry at that person because there are no delusions in their mind and therefore no cause of anger. Similarly, a higher bodhisattva, who has totally renounced the self and only cherishes others, cannot become angry. With the new bodhisattva, there might be a flash of anger due to past imprints, but it is very rare and doesn't last more than a second.

This shows us that the other person's harm is not the main cause of anger. If it were, then anger *must* arise—whatever the level of mind of the person being harmed. But really the harm is only a condition; the main cause, the imprint of anger from previous moments of anger, is already on the mind. Until we have completely removed the imprint of anger, there is always the chance it will ripen and anger will arise. Therefore we must always protect our mind; we must be constantly aware of our thoughts and able to avert any negative thought that might arise.

This is the first of the two main reasons why we get angry—we have not removed the imprint of anger, or the other delusions, from our mindstream by generating the remedy of the path. The imprint is like the seed that can always sprout into a full-grown plant with the right conditions such as earth, water, and sun. If we have the seed of anger within our mindstream, there is little we can do to stop it when the conditions come together. Every time we become angry, we leave an imprint on our mind that will cause us to become angry in the future, thus perpetuating and increasing our anger. The more negative imprints of anger we leave, the more difficult our future life will be. However, when we directly realize emptiness on the path of seeing, we finally destroy the seeds of the disturbing-thought obscurations (*nyondrib*) and cease all gross delusions such as anger, attachment, jealousy, and so forth, making it impossible for any delusion to arise. But even before removing the seeds entirely, we can avert anger by applying the remedies to anger that we have learned in our Dharma practice.

The second reason anger arises is that despite knowing the remedies, we do not apply them. The Kadampa geshes say that meditating on a deity is easy, but practicing the Dharma is difficult. We can do a deity practice and recite lots of mantras but, unless we transform everything we do into Dharma, we will never have realizations. We can relate that here to patience. Unless we let go of clinging to this life, everything we do will be nonvirtuous, and anger will arise so easily when our desires are frustrated. Only by practicing patience can we change that.

How we view a situation depends entirely on our mind. Viewed one way, the person wanting to harm us is an enemy, and the action is a harmful one. Viewed another way, that person is a friend, and their action is helpful. It is like having the choice to switch channels on our TV to a violent movie or a gentle one. Just as our mind is the door to all suffering, it is also the door to all happiness, depending on how we use it. Because present happiness and present suffering depend on what attitude we have, we must constantly watch our mind, always keeping it virtuous.

Whenever we face an angry person and have the opportunity to practice patience, we should do it. To not practice patience while that person is there is to miss a great opportunity. Just as we say "an apple a day keeps the doctor away," we can say "some patience a day keeps the lower realms away." That's how important it is in our life, and we should never miss the opportunity to practice it. We should persist, even if we often fail. It is very difficult at the beginning. We might be able to remain patient for a few seconds, and then our patience is gone. But over the years we will certainly improve if we work on it consistently.

Without controlling our anger, we lose the incredible chance at happiness. That loss is incalculable; it is so much worse than losing a million dollars, or even a billion dollars. Perhaps we get angry at an enemy and make them give us a billion dollars. We are richer by a billion dollars, but we must face eons of the most terrible suffering in the lower realms because of that anger, without a cent, without a rag to cover us or a scrap of food.

THE DISADVANTAGES OF ANGER

Anger and patience are dichotomies; when one is present in our mind, the other cannot be. Therefore being angry blocks the chance of being patient and is a great hindrance to developing bodhichitta. Anger is the mind that wishes to harm the other being—that is its function— whereas bodhichitta is the opposite.

Along with heresy, anger is considered the most damaging mind to have, in that it destroys any undedicated merit. Just as grain that is completely burned in a fire can never sprout into the plant, any positive merit we have can never ripen into a positive result when burned by anger or heresy.

In *A Guide to the Bodhisattva's Way of Life*, Shantideva said,

> [A moment of] ill-will destroys all good deeds,
> as well as generosity and worship of the sugatas,
> even if one has practiced them
> for thousands of cosmic cycles.[44]

Merit that has been dedicated will not be completely burned, but the result will still be disturbed; for instance, it may become impossible to experience the result for a thousand eons. All our realizations on the path—even our temporal happiness—will be delayed for that incredible length of time.

Whenever we have the slightest anger arising in our mind, we must do whatever we can to avert it. The moment before anger arises we can be sitting comfortably and contentedly, just relaxing, and then, suddenly, right away, there is anger, completely destroying the sense of peace and happiness we were experiencing. Suddenly there is great pain in our heart as the flame of anger flares up, destroying this moment's peace and destroying our future happiness.

Virtue is very rare, like the lightning in the sky, whereas our mind is like the nighttime without the moon or the stars—completely dark. We can generate a virtuous thought very occasionally, and then only for the briefest moment. If that is so, how can we then destroy that precious virtuous thought by becoming angry? We must be so careful to watch our mind and never allow anger to arise, as if we are walking along a narrow path on the edge of a high cliff that we could plummet over at any moment if we let our guard slip.

At nighttime we go to bed with anger; in the morning we get up with anger. During the entire day we live our life with anger, accumulating so much negative karma, feeling physically uncomfortable and deriving no pleasure from the things around us. The most luxurious house gives us no happiness; the most delicious food seems tasteless while we have anger.

Perhaps we have faith in the Dharma, talking about it often with our friends, but when we are overcome with anger, all that Dharma is forgotten. What we have learned about karma, refuge, or any of the other subjects seems very far away. Consumed with anger, there is great danger.

Bodhisattvas are not like that at all. Because their only thought is to be of benefit to all sentient beings, even if somebody harms them they would never wish to retaliate. A bodhisattva will always give help in return for harm. This is the opposite of our behavior; we are always looking for our own interests and so will harm others, regardless of whether they have helped or harmed us. Because of the amazing mind of bodhichitta, a bodhisattva only feels great bliss no matter what happens. Therefore there is no such thing as "harm" as we know it.

Although anger always looks to an external enemy to blame, we must see that it is only ever the inner enemy, our self-cherishing, that produces our anger. This is what destroys all our merit and creates such suffering for ourselves and others.

Extinguishing the Fuel of Anger

There is nothing pleasant at all about anger. Irritation, agitation, impatience, sullenness, spite—all these sorts of negative emotions overwhelm us and refuse to give us one moment's peace, whereas when we have patience, we have genuine peace. There is no question of which is preferable. The frustrated, unhappy mind is the fuel that can easily grow into anger. Until we have learned to overcome that anger with patience, it will destroy any happiness we have.

It's not that anger and hatred are weak minds. With hatred our mind is incredibly focused on the object of our hatred and how to destroy it. We should turn that strength around to destroy the real enemy, focusing all our attention on what is really causing us such unhappiness—our own anger. We need to destroy it completely with patience.

We don't have to become angry when an enemy tries to harm us or when adverse situations occur. It's impossible to avoid problems, but when we analyze such situations, we will see that there is no reason for becoming unhappy. Unless we can generate a happy mind, how can we renounce the unhappy one? We therefore need to think well on the benefits of voluntarily accepting suffering and make a strong determination to not allow anger and frustration to arise, no matter what happens around us.

It is very easy to let a day go by without practicing patience, then a week, a month, a year. Before we know it, our whole life has gone and then, suddenly, unexpectedly, death happens and we have never developed patience in our mind, despite all the teachings we have studied and retreats we have done. At the time of death it's too late to regret not developing patience.

What we can do now in a very practical way is to watch our mind, and the moment it is disturbed by somebody or something, by understanding the terrible effects of anger, we determine to not allow even a moment of anger to arise. We can make a plan to do this for a certain time each day and gradually increase it. If we train our mind in patience in that way, doing whatever we can to overcome any angry thought that arises, by keeping at it, change will definitely happen, year by year. Seeing how there is so much more peace now that the angry mind does not arise gives us the determination to practice patience even more. Then, thinking back on how we once would have become angry from one sharp word from a colleague at work or from the noise of branches tapping on our window disturbing our sleep, we will wonder why we ever got so angry. It is just a matter of practice.

The Three Types of Patience

The general definition of patience is being able to forbear any harm or difficulty inflicted by others. Specifically, there are three types of patience:

1. The patience of disregarding the harm done by others
2. The patience of accepting suffering
3. The patience of gaining certainty about the Dharma

How much happiness and peace of mind there is in our everyday life depends on how much we are able to practice these three types of patience. Therefore it is very important to not only understand precisely what they are but also to practice them.

For instance, we might have done many retreats and have a daily meditation practice that includes lots of mantra recitation, and we really think we are becoming a better person, but suddenly, when something bad happens and somebody harms us in some way, we immediately want to retaliate. That indicates that something fundamental is missing in our practice. If such a situation happens, we should think, "If I get angry, what have I been doing? All these offerings I make, all these prostrations I do, all these practices are to subdue my mind and destroy my delusions, so it makes no sense to become angry while trying to do all this. What a childish, crazy thing to do. By getting angry I will be destroying everything I have been working for."

1. The Patience of Disregarding the Harm Done by Others

The first type of patience is the patience of disregarding the harm done by others, of not retaliating when faced with harm.

Without patience, no matter how much education we have, there is no peace or freedom at all. Our mind becomes the servant to our anger, completely under its control. The sole reason we have given ourselves an education is to be happy, and yet if we don't have a good heart, nothing will bring us peace and happiness—nothing will protect our mind from suffering or from its causes: ignorance and dissatisfaction.

There are many reasons why anger is inappropriate. Although it is natural to think when we are harmed in some way that we are blameless and the other person is entirely to blame, that is not so. Their action might seem volitional but really they have no control; they are ruled by their delusions. Of this Shantideva said,

> I myself during my past lives brought similar torments
> upon other beings. Therefore it is only fitting
> that this same tribulation should fall upon me,
> who am the cause of injury to other living beings.
>
> His sword and my body are the twofold cause of my pain.
> He bears the sword,
> I, the body,
> with which one should I feel angry?
>
> In the shape of a body I adopted this open sore,
> sensitive to the slightest touch.
> If I myself, blinded by thirst, bring upon it further affliction,
> what should be the object of my anger?[45]

Of course, when somebody is beating us with a stick, we blame the person. Being angry at a stick is complete nonsense because it is under the control of the person. When we look deeper, however, we can see that the person too is being controlled. Utterly overwhelmed by anger, they have no freedom at all. If there is anything to blame, it is their anger, the delusion that forces them to act harmfully and create negative karma. Therefore they are not an object of hatred and blame but of compassion, used as they are like a slave by their anger. Thinking this way, rather than thinking about our own happiness and how it is being harmed, we have no choice but to feel deep compassion for them. We see the other person as so pitiful, with so much suffering.

But we should look even deeper for the cause of our harm. The only reason we are experiencing that harm at all is because we have created the cause in the first place. If that is so, then it's only right that we now must face the results.

According to our self-cherishing, it is perfectly acceptable to treat the other person badly (they totally deserve it) but utterly unacceptable that we are treated badly in any way (we are totally blameless). When we understand karma, however, we can see that there is no way we can be harmed by that person without having created the cause for that harm through having harmed them in the past. This is just the ripening of some past karma; we have created the cause and we are experiencing the result. When we accept this, the situation does not become a problem. On top of this, it gives us space to generate compassion for that person. We only want to help them, to protect them from creating negative karma.

From the person's side, because of what we did to them in the past, they have been forced to create negative karma and will have to face the consequences. Their negative karma will block them from another human rebirth, causing them instead to be reborn in the lower realms where they will experience the most terrible suffering.

Without an Enemy There Is No Chance to Practice Patience
We must realize that even if all the people in the world were angry with us—even if they killed us—we are just one living being, just one person being hurt, but if we—that one person—fail to practice patience, then numberless other beings will receive harm from us, and that is much more dangerous. Right now, at this moment, we have the choice whether to practice patience or practice anger. We have this opportunity to give all beings peace and happiness. Therefore we need to develop patience, and for that we need those who try to harm us.

Shantideva said,

> If I think he should not have my respect
> thinking that my enemy's intention is to harm me,
> how would I otherwise practice forgiveness?
> Would I practice forgiveness toward, say, a physician whose
>   goal is my own good?[46]

Unless somebody opposes us in some way, there is no way we can practice patience. Somebody who tries to help us, like a doctor, cannot serve that purpose. Even though the Buddha and all the gurus have taught us everything we need to know about developing patience, because they have no anger toward us, we have no opportunity to practice it with them. The best type of sentient being we can practice patience with is the enemy, the one who abuses or tries to harm us in some way. Once we understand the need to develop patience, we will see that we need somebody like that. Our virtuous teacher might have given us the teachings, but this person we call an enemy is the one who allows us to put those teachings into practice and, in that way, is also a virtuous teacher.

If their animosity lasted years and years, we would have so long to practice on them. However, their anger at us will probably not last that long. It is not permanent; it will soon disappear. In another hour they may no longer be angry at us. They certainly won't be angry at us in a hundred years' time, so there will be no chance to practice patience then. *Right now* is the only opportunity we have to practice patience. If we don't manage to develop patience while that person is still angry at us, when can we? We cannot miss such a wonderful opportunity.

An enemy criticizes us, whereas a friend praises us; we don't want criticism, whereas we always welcome praise. We should consider this. When we are praised we naturally feel proud, and pride is a great obstacle to developing the mind. The various results of pride are explained in the teachings on karma. We are blocked from learning and from attaining realizations, and it stops our ability to benefit others. It causes us to be born in the lower realms or, at the least, as poor or blind. By criticizing us, the enemy harms our pride, which damages our self-cherishing. Because self-cherishing is the sole source of all our suffering, in doing that our enemy is the sole source of all our peace and happiness, all the way up to enlightenment. The chance our enemy offers us to practice patience is like the medicine we have in our house in case of emergency, such as a heart attack; in fact, taking the medicine of patience is ultimately far more important than taking medicine for the body.

That person's action appears harmful to us, and we believe that label to be completely true. Having labeled it a harmful action, believing that label, we then act on the anger that arises because of it, creating nonvirtue and future suffering. When we change the label and see the action as helpful, the thought of anger does not arise. Instead of giving victory to our anger and becoming its slave, we give ourselves freedom.

What we need to do is turn the situation around and see how that person has given us the chance to develop our patience further. From that perspective, they have taught us the most valuable lesson and are therefore the most kind, the most precious one. If we think in this way, the kindness they have shown us is inexpressible. This "enemy" is the guru who helps us on the path, allowing us to attain bodhichitta and enlightenment. As Langri Tangpa said in *Eight Verses on Mind Training*,

> Even if one whom I have helped,
> or in whom I have placed great hope,
> gravely mistreats me in hurtful ways,
> I will train myself to view him as my sublime teacher.[47]

With No More Anger There Are No More Enemies

The number of enemies we have and the amount of harm we receive depend on the strength of our anger. When we are free from anger, we are free from enemies. Arya bodhisattvas receive no harm at all from others because they have eliminated all delusions.

With anger, it is very easy to find external enemies; without it, it is impossible. If we have the concept of an enemy, we see an enemy; if we don't have the concept of an enemy, we don't see an enemy. Without anger, even if all sentient beings were to become angry with us, criticize us, or even kill us, from our side we could not find even one enemy among them. This enemy is the view of our negative thoughts, an interpretation, a label. It's not the view of all our minds. It's not the view of our positive, pure minds. We need to change our view, not eliminate all the external enemies.

As Shantideva said,

> Where will you find enough leather
> to cover the whole earth?
> Merely by wearing a pair of leather shoes
> you will cover the earth.

> In the same way,
> since I cannot control external objects,
> I will control my own mind.
> What is there to gain by controlling the rest?[48]

Imagine if, before a world trip, we told our friends we were buying many millions of square miles of leather to cover the entire surface of the planet so we could travel without getting thorns in our feet. People would think we were crazy. The earth is vast, and our feet are tiny. Rather than covering the earth with leather, all we need to do to protect ourselves is to buy some shoes. In exactly the same way, rather than having to protect ourselves from the external thorns of our enemies' harm, we protect our mind with patience and awareness. Then no matter how many atomic bombs our enemy might have, they can never harm us. Without anger, there can be no harm. While overcoming our anger might be hard, it is possible, whereas being free from all external enemies without destroying our anger is impossible.

Therefore it is vital that we attack our real enemy, the self-cherishing mind that generates negative thoughts such as anger, rather than those we currently consider our enemies. Worldly people see the victor in a bloody battle as a hero and call them brave, but the one who actually qualifies for the title "hero," the one who is truly brave, is the one who fights the inner enemy, defeating the self-cherishing mind and its army of disturbing thoughts. Although the common warrior might kill other human beings, they are only killing corpses. We are all "living corpses" because we are in these bodies for such a short time, so whether we are victor or vanquished is of little consequence; a battle is nothing more than a fight between two corpses.

Since beginningless time we have followed the dictates of our self-cherishing, and all it has ever brought us is endless suffering. When we are harmed in some way, we have two choices: to follow the self-cherishing and harm the harmer in return, or to practice patience and overcome our self-cherishing.

When we reach the stage when we can actually feel the kindness of the person who harms us, there will be deep joy and peace. This is something we can't purchase from a department store or a supermarket, even if we had a billion dollars. This is the importance of the enemy, the one who doesn't love us but instead has anger for us, and who criticizes and abuses us.

2. The Patience of Accepting Suffering

The second of the three types of patience is the patience of voluntarily accepting suffering. When we reflect deeply on our life, we will see how while we remain in this unenlightened state, it is not only unavoidable to experience suffering but also completely natural. We should see that the nature of whatever we experience with our unsubdued mind is only suffering, regardless of whether it is a pleasant, unpleasant, or neutral feeling.

Furthermore, we should analyze those feelings in order to understand how we see them as permanent and independent, whereas they are not; all those feelings of anger, attachment, and indifference are impermanent—they arise, last a while, and go—and are dependent on causes and conditions. They are empty of being the independent entities they seem to be.

In the *Lamrim Chenmo*, Lama Tsongkhapa explained that when we become unhappy, angry, or paranoid (actually, he didn't say paranoid—I just added that), we should see how all negative emotions arise because we have this container of contaminated aggregates, this body and mind. Just as somebody carrying a heavy load cannot be happy until they have put down that load, we cannot find real happiness until we have unburdened ourselves of the contaminated aggregates.[49]

To explore this, I recommend regularly reading the chapters on patience and wisdom in Shantideva's *A Guide to the Bodhisattva's Way of Life*. The entire chapter on patience shows us the disadvantages of anger and the advantages of patience, and the entire chapter on wisdom shows us how things dependently arise and are empty of inherent existence. These two chapters combined are the best cure for the deluded minds that cause suffering now. In fact, they are the best study of psychology.[50] Thought-transformation texts are also very effective for the mind, giving us an infallible method to meet and overcome any thoughts of frustration or anger that arise. Studying these texts is not like doing a university degree that only brings some limited benefit after years of study; studying for even one day brings great benefit.

Why Be Unhappy?

There is no reason to become unhappy with any undesirable situation, either ones we can resolve or ones we cannot. Shantideva said,

> If there is a solution,
> what good is discontent.

> If there is no solution,
> what good is it anyway?[51]

This verse should be remembered at all times because it gives us the reason we should never be unhappy; it is so effective for the mind. If there is a possibility to resolve the problem, we should attempt to do just that. What is the point of being unhappy when we see we can fix it? We are just causing difficulties for ourselves by clinging to unhappiness when the solution is right there in front of us. As soon as we start to resolve the situation, the reason for our unhappiness disappears.

Perhaps the situation cannot be resolved. If that is so, what is the point of being unhappy? It's useless. Say, in a book on Buddhist psychology, we read a definition of space as "that which is empty of resistance." Because we really dislike the fact that there can be something empty of resistance, we don't like this definition. However, that is the reality; there is absolutely nothing we can do about it. So how absurd it is to become angry about it. There is not the slightest benefit from wishing that it might be otherwise.

This advice becomes particularly important when something major happens in our life. If we go for a checkup and our doctor tells us we have cancer, how do we deal with it? Although there is nothing we can do to change the situation, at least we can change our attitude to the situation. Rather than becoming totally depressed, we can see that here is an amazing opportunity to transform our mind. Other people have no thought of the impermanence of life, and so they waste this incredibly precious life. We, on the other hand, are aware of how little time we have, and so we must make the most of every minute. Then, because we know from our own situation that the thought of dying with cancer can cause great anxiety, we have great sympathy for those in the same situation. When we encounter somebody with cancer, we want them to be free from that misery with all our heart. From that compassion comes the wish to benefit them in whatever way we can, and so we dedicate our life to alleviating the suffering of those with cancer.

I have seen this many times with people who have a particular disease such as cancer or AIDS. Somebody who doesn't have the same disease might feel sorry for the sick person but will not have the same degree of compassion and empathy. Many, of course, turn away, rejecting the person through fear of the disease. There is a psychological difference between somebody who shares the problem and somebody who doesn't.

Clinging to an unrealizable goal brings so many problems, so the solution is to stop the clinging. In such situations where there is nothing we can do, it is good to practice rejoicing. Say our partner has left us for another person. Rather than be driven mad with jealousy, depression, and misery, we can feel that they did what was best for them and they are making themselves and their new partner happy. Although we cannot remedy the situation, by seeing it in this light we use it to create positive karma that will result in happiness in the future.

Rather than feeling jealous of those who have what we cannot have, we can rejoice in their good fortune. When somebody has success at work or in the Dharma, or they have a wonderful house, luxurious possessions, or plenty of friends, whereas we haven't, we should simply rejoice for that person and not feel jealous. Jealousy interferes with our future success, so it not only makes us miserable now but also in the future.

We will have to face problems until we have overcome the whole of samsara. We will continue to be harmed by other beings and by circumstances such as aging or illness. As long as our mind is conditioned to identify such experiences as problems, more and more things will be problems to us. The smallest, most insignificant matter will cause great pain in our mind and we will become upset very quickly. On the other hand, if we see undesirable conditions as beneficial, we will be happy. The more we see the benefits of facing problems positively, the happier we will be to experience them.

We should make the strong determination that we will regard whatever we encounter as a cause for happiness rather than as a problem. There is simply no reason to be irritated by something. The situation itself has no power to disturb our mind; it's how we react to it. Therefore we should reflect extensively about the shortcomings of always expecting things to go our way and the advantages of using unfavorable situations as a means to develop our mind.

Training our mind in this way, we become like somebody who has learned to ride a horse well. No matter how fast the horse gallops or how erratic it is, they always remain safely in the saddle, never in danger of falling off. With a well-trained mind, we never fall into depression or misery; even if our mind is distracted, we are still able to cope. And just as a good rider will enjoy a rough ride, we will learn to see a challenging situation as a great opportunity. Without any effort, the thought of enjoying problems will come, like the thought of enjoying ice cream. Or just as somebody who loves music will feel so happy when hearing a tune, we will be happy whenever we encounter a problem. Whatever happens—criticism, poverty, sickness, even death—we will only think, "This is good."

Accepting problems rather than rejecting them can make a big difference to our experience, reducing our worry and fear and turning our actions into the Dharma. By showing us how all samsara is only suffering, our problems can help us develop renunciation. And when we recognize their emptiness, we can use them as a means to develop wisdom, something not possible when we are overcome with attachment. In that way, problems become the best possible teaching.

This is the essence of the Mahayana thought training. Whenever we encounter a problem, rather than feeling aversion for it, we can use it to give us a stronger sense of refuge in the Buddha, Dharma, and Sangha; to eliminate our pride; to purify our negative karma; to practice virtue; and to train our mind in compassion and loving-kindness.[52]

Everything Becomes Easier with Acquaintance
When we train our mind to bear suffering, it becomes progressively easier. Of this Shantideva said,

> There is nothing that will remain difficult after practice,
> therefore, if I first practice
> with less severe afflictions,
> even the greatest torments will become bearable.[53]

Whether something is easy or difficult depends on how well acquainted we are with it. Say we have been living with bugs—fleas, bedbugs, and so forth—for a long time. This becomes normal for us. Fleas in our clothes, nits in our hair—they don't bother us at all after a while. On the other hand, if we have never come across bugs before, to encounter bugs for the first time is a great shock. We want the fleas in our house killed or we want to buy a new house!

For somebody without patience, even small irritations are very disturbing; they always find so many discomforts and harms, and their impatience increases. We sometimes see this with old people who find fault everywhere. If they are staying in a care home, they complain about everything: the food is terrible, the place is noisy, the staff never clean, there is no garden—on and on. While for others there are no problems at all, for these people nothing is ever right. This happens when the mind is too concerned with the happiness of the self, when there is strong self-cherishing. Such a person can easily become paranoid.

When we have a mind that is easily irritated, the weather is either too hot or too cold, too rainy or too windy. Wrapped up in our own selfish happiness in that way, the suffering we experience when facing these small harms will grow. The more we are used to only sleeping in a big, soft bed, the more unbearable a small, hard bed will seem. If we could be a little patient and learn to bear it, the harm would stop increasing. In accepting the uncomfortable bed one night, it becomes progressively easier to sleep in it the following nights. In this way, slowly our ability to withstand discomfort increases.

By practicing the patience of voluntarily accepting suffering, when we start with small harms, such as bearing the heat of a summer's day or being criticized, we will later be able to bear greater harms. Eventually we will be able to accept the fires of the hells voluntarily in order to save even one sentient being or, like Guru Shakyamuni Buddha, give our life willingly to starving tigers.

We worldly people work incredibly hard and have great patience for our mundane concerns. It takes a lot of effort to acquire possessions, prestige, and so forth. From a Dharma point of view, all that hard work seems utterly pointless. On the other hand, to obtain the happiness of future lives, liberation from samsara, and enlightenment, a Dharma practitioner willingly accepts suffering. The more we train our mind, the more patience we develop, until there will be no problems no matter what happens, even if we meet great suffering.

If we can't control our anger, it doesn't matter what good advice on patience we receive; we either disagree with it or find it very difficult to follow. Perhaps a teacher explained about the kindness of the enemy. We might have agreed in theory but decided that that only applies to people who harm us in trivial ways, whereas this particular enemy is completely bad, completely wrong, and the teaching doesn't apply to us. The teacher must have been talking about some other enemy!

Bearing hardships with patience is especially important for somebody practicing the Dharma. We can't expect to do a retreat, for instance, without facing any problems. If we wait to start the retreat until everything is perfect, until we never have to endure any discomfort, the retreat will never get done. When we are too concerned with comfort, even our daily practice becomes weaker because of all the frustrations in our mind, becoming shorter until we no longer do it.

On the other hand, by slowly developing our patience, the problems that upset us in the past no longer do. Over years of training in patience we will see how our mind changes. Whereas a few years back anger arose so easily, many times a day, now it no longer does, even if we have received terrible harm. We could be scolded, beaten, starved, and our mind would remain patient and happy.

Patience results not only in our own happiness and well-being but also in the happiness and well-being of countless others. The many wars that were fought in the last century and are still being fought are due to greed, hatred, and intolerance, all stemming from ego. With patience, this could never happen. Even on a domestic level, patience is the vital element in bringing harmony and happiness to a couple, a family, and a community. When we practice patience and accept suffering voluntarily, we become an inspiration to others.

3. The Patience of Gaining Certainty about the Dharma

The third type of patience is the patience of gaining certainty about the Dharma. We do this by meditating on and understanding the meaning of the lamrim, understanding and appreciating the extraordinary qualities of the Three Rare Sublime Ones (the Buddha, Dharma, and Sangha), being convinced of the crucial importance of attaining enlightenment, and having certainty about the effectiveness of the path that leads there. When we have all these qualities, then we will never lack the patience to persevere with our Dharma practice.

When we conscientiously try to follow the ways of the bodhisattva in order to attain bodhichitta because of our deep wish to benefit all sentient beings, then we will surely do whatever we need to do in order to progress to enlightenment. This will naturally lead to enduring whatever hardships we may encounter and transforming our attitude toward whoever we now consider an enemy. We should constantly remind ourselves of the need for not just a little patience but the perfection of patience, and we should pray that we can reach the very highest attainment of patience quickly. By considering such a practice as a vital aspect of our training, we will definitely be able to overcome all difficulties and attain the perfection of patience.

THE DETERMINATION TO DEVELOP PATIENCE

Whatever way we look at it, we will see there is no justification for anger and every reason to do whatever we can to fully develop our patience. Then compassion rather than anger will arise for whoever tries to harm us. It might seem that we are an impatient person and there is nothing we can do about it. We might see others who have a lot of patience and feel we can never be like that, but we must understand what Shantideva said: everything becomes easier with acquaintance. By training our mind we can definitely develop patience.

At present, the opposite naturally happens. Somebody harms us and we dwell on that harm, allowing our anger to grow, going over their harm again and again. Even if we are lying in bed trying to sleep, we can't relax at all, dwelling on what we can do to them, dreaming of ways of making them nonexistent. We might even decide to jump up and phone them to tell them what we think of them. In that way, we train our mind in perfecting our anger.

In just the same way, we can train our mind in patience and compassion, thinking over all the reasons that person is so kind, so precious. Just as a negative mind can arise in our mind due to certain imprints and conditions, a positive mind can arise. Because of its impermanent nature, any negative mind can be diminished and eliminated. For exactly the same reason, any positive mind can be developed and perfected. Through training, we can definitely generate patience, loving-kindness, and compassion whenever we sense an angry thought about to arise. In this way we can reduce our habit of becoming angry.

Some people feel that getting angry is often useful, that we need to be furious in order to have the energy to change a bad situation. Say a neighbor is always noisy, playing music very loudly very late. We might think the only way to get them to stop is to confront them and angrily demand they stop. I think there is always another way to change a bad situation without getting angry. We can do something, but do it with patience, loving-kindness, and compassion.

The Kadampa geshe Ben Gungyal was a great Tibetan meditator.[54] When he was training his mind, every evening before going to bed he had a pile of white stones and a pile of black stones. He checked how many virtuous and how many nonvirtuous actions he had done that day, placing one white stone in one pile for every virtuous action and one black stone in the other pile for every nonvirtuous action. At the beginning there were very few white stones and many black ones, but as he persevered with his meditations, the pile of white ones grew and the pile of black ones diminished. Finally, there were more white than black.

We may do our best not to get angry, but we still do, and then we get angry at ourselves for getting angry! I think this is where regret is very useful. Rather than feeling hopeless, thinking we can never change, we can see that we tried and failed this time and regret having become angry. We can then make the firm resolve to try again—and again and again—until we start to control our anger. The stronger our regret, the more determination we will have to change.

Patience is a quality that we can learn. We spend a lot of time and energy learning about another country's customs and language. If we can put so much effort into something like that, why shouldn't we learn patience? This is the *most* important thing we can learn, so we should put great effort into it.

Practicing patience is not just for the person seeking enlightenment for the sake of all sentient beings; it is not just for the person seeking liberation from samsara or the happiness of future lives. Anybody—religious or nonreligious—who wants harmony in their relationships, who wants happiness and friendship, who wants love and contentment, needs patience.

4 : PERSEVERANCE

The Mind That Rejoices in Virtue

THE PERFECTION of perseverance, or joyous perseverance, is also called the perfection of enthusiasm or energy. In Sanskrit it is *virya* and in Tibetan it is *tsöndrü*. Like the other perfections, it is a vital quality we need to develop. In *A Guide to the Bodhisattva's Way of Life*, Shantideva said,

> One who practices patience in the above way should develop
>   fortitude.
> For awakening depends on fortitude;
> because, without fortitude there is no merit,
> as there is no movement without wind.
>
> What is fortitude?
> It is persevering effort in the cultivation of virtue.[55]

At present, we attempt to find happiness in mundane pleasure, and because of that we are always disappointed. Moreover, in our attempt, we create nonvirtue. Here Shantideva showed us that happiness is the complete opposite of this, that happiness lies in creating virtue. When we see this, we will naturally want to do virtuous things and we will find joy in doing them. When that happens we will have boundless energy to do more virtuous things. This is enthusiastic or joyous perseverance.

We Need Correct Practice as Well as Perseverance

Working for mundane happiness requires great, sustained effort. People such as butchers work long hours at very difficult physical labor, tirelessly accumulating negative karma by killing beings for money. Similarly, people stay out in terrible conditions—in heat, cold, and rain—fishing all day long, just so they can kill living beings for fun. Soldiers train under extreme conditions in order to be skilled at killing the enemy. People risk their lives to gain a good reputation or beat a competitor in business. Everywhere we look, people are working so hard creating nonvirtue to ensure a rebirth in the lower realms.

Perseverance must be correct perseverance; it must be persevering in doing positive actions, accumulating merit. From our side, we must develop perseverance but also ensure that we don't cheat the holy Dharma by practicing incorrectly. With a correct understanding and correct application of the Dharma as the foundation, by persevering in the right practice we will certainly succeed. It is entirely in our hands.

We should work even more strenuously than the butchers, the fishers, or the soldiers, but for a positive reason: to destroy our delusions. If perseverance in a Dharma sense is rejoicing in virtue, we should joyfully endure whatever hardships we encounter in order to develop our mind. When others get angry with us or criticize us, when we are treated badly, we should be able to happily bear the hardships, because this is how we best train in the path to enlightenment.

In *Heart-Instructions of The Book of Kadam*, Yongzin Yeshé Gyaltsen attributed Lama Atisha[56] as saying,

> Just as any crops can grow when the soil is fertile,
> In a good heart all higher qualities arise as wished for;
> Whatever you do must be enforced by the awakening mind;
> So stated Atisha to the spiritual mentor Dromtönpa.
>
> One whose mind is stable and diligent has no obstacles;
> One who is versed in what is allowed and what is proscribed
>   goes to liberation.
> Thus, learning, discipline, and kindness must complement
>   each other;
> this is most important, said the most excellent lord.[57]

Atisha started with the example of the field. If it is well plowed and well cultivated, then whatever is planted there will grow well. In the same way, if we have a good heart, then all our wishes will be attained; everything we wish for will happen. With perseverance there will be no obstacles to any happiness, especially to ultimate happiness, the freedom from the oceans of samsaric suffering, and peerless happiness, the state of the omniscient mind. I myself am lazy, but those who have perseverance have no obstacles. Whatever they want to achieve can be achieved.

There is a Tibetan saying that a turtle goes very, very slowly but reaches its goal, whereas a flea jumps all over the place but never gets anywhere. Somebody who is active for a short time—that is, someone who has a little perseverance but not enough—will not succeed. I think this saying is very useful.

Continuity is so important. We shouldn't practice for a short while but then, due to lack of perseverance, give up because the mind has become weaker. Then maybe, after having stopped for a long time, we meet somebody or hear a talk and become inspired again, causing us to try again for a few days or a few months. It should not be like that. Even though the Dharma practice we do might be very small, it is most important to persevere with it.

We need concentration to develop on the path to enlightenment, and we need perseverance to overcome the obstacles to attaining perfect concentration. Without perseverance, even if we try to concentrate, we are trapped in the disturbed mind, distracted by either sinking or scattering thoughts, like being caught between the fangs of a vicious animal. Shantideva said,

> Having developed fortitude in this way,
> the bodhisattva should establish his mind in concentration,
> for a person whose is distracted
> is trapped in the jaws of the afflictions.[58]

We need perseverance, and we need to know what should be practiced and what should be abandoned. Learning, discipline, and kindness are so important. When we know the Dharma, we can develop the wisdom to discriminate right from wrong in this life. Then we can abandon what is wrong and practice what is right and, because of that, reach the blissful state of peace.

THE THREE TYPES OF PERSEVERANCE

There are three types of perseverance:

1. Armor-like perseverance
2. The perseverance of gathering virtue
3. The perseverance of working for the welfare of others

1. Armor-Like Perseverance

Seeing how all our happiness and suffering come from the mind, we must guard the mind at all times. In *Opening the Door of Dharma*, Lodrö Gyaltsen said,

> What is the use of any conduct apart from the conduct of protecting the mind?[59]

This is very good to remember in our daily life. Even though we may do hundreds of other things, if we leave out this most important practice we cannot stop our problems and achieve happiness, especially ultimate happiness.

In *A Guide to the Bodhisattva's Way of Life*, Shantideva said,

> He who would keep the precepts
> should watch the mind diligently;
> a person who does not watch the unstable mind
> cannot keep the precepts.
>
> Wild elephants in rut do not cause
> in this world the damage

that the elephant of an unrestrained mind
will cause in the avici hell and all the other hells.

However, if the elephant of the mind
is well tied with the rope of mindfulness,
all danger vanishes,
all good is within our reach.[60]

Unless we protect our mind, what is the use of doing all the other things we do in life? The mind is habituated to nonvirtue; when the mind is unprotected, it will naturally go in that direction. Then, twenty-four hours a day, our life will be under the control of the self-cherishing mind, doing negative actions caused by the three poisons. Every single action of body, speech, and mind becomes negative karma, being the cause of not only future samsara but also the most unbearable suffering of the three lower realms.

However, when the crazy elephant mind is firmly bound by the rope of mindfulness, all fears, all dangers are stopped, and all virtues come into our hands, meaning we can easily attain all the realizations of the path to enlightenment, all the way up to enlightenment.

In *Friendly Letter*, speaking to the king the letter is addressed to, Nagarjuna said,

O Fearless One, what need to tell you more,
for here's the counsel that will truly help:
the vital point is to tame your mind, for mind's
the root of the Dharma, so the Buddha said.[61]

This relates directly to the essential teaching of the Buddha:

Do not perform any nonvirtuous actions,
perform only virtuous actions,
subdue your mind thoroughly—
this is the teaching of the Buddha.[62]

Subduing our mind is the very essence of the Dharma. We can do many practices to help us develop our mind, but the essential practice is not harming others—living in morality. That means that in our everyday life we bind the mind with the practice of mindfulness, overcoming any nonvirtuous thoughts and only developing virtuous ones. Like taking medicine when our body is sick, when we are aware of any nonvirtuous thought arising in our mind, we take the medicine of Dharma to avert it, applying the appropriate antidote.

When we protect our mind, we are protected from external harm. Of this, Shantideva said,

> Tigers, lions, elephants, bears,
> poisonous snakes and all human enemies,
> and in addition all the jailers of hell,
> as well as dakinis and rakshasas,
>
> all of them become restrained
> by merely restraining the mind,
> and by merely taming the mind
> they all become tame.
>
> For He Who Speaks the Truth has said
> that all the dangers
> and the countless sorrows of the world
> arise from the mind.[63]

No negative karma can ripen when we guard our mind, and so no harm can come to us. By not letting our mind be controlled by delusions, we don't create negative karma, and so, of course, we don't have to experience the negative result.

For example, Devadatta, the Buddha's cousin, was very jealous of the Buddha and always tried to compete with and harm him. One day, when the Buddha was begging for alms, Devadatta sent a crazy elephant to attack him. However, instead of harming him, the elephant became completely subdued when it came into the presence of the Buddha. There is a similar story about how the Italian saint Francis of Assisi subdued a wolf through his great compassion. I also heard that mosquitoes never bit His Holiness Zong Rinpoche.[64]

Tying the mind to virtue, protecting it from delusions, means we don't create negative karma, so there are no dangers to our life. Also, because of bodhichitta, our mind is subdued. Tying our mind to virtue and away from disturbing thoughts is like tying up all dangerous beings: tigers, snakes, hell guardians, and all our enemies. Due to the power of bodhichitta we are even able to control the elements.

These verses are very important to remember whenever you feel depressed. There are many reasons for feeling down, such as being unable to go on retreat because of family obligations or finding it difficult to learn the Dharma. To stop depression or other negative minds, it would be very good to write down these quotations and maybe make cards of them. You can hang them on the walls in your home to encourage you and keep your mind happy.

Perseverance means keeping at it despite the hardships. Guru Shakyamuni Buddha collected merit for three countless great eons before he attained enlightenment, sacrificing himself for other sentient beings by giving away his limbs, his eyes, and even his entire body. For three countless great eons he practiced morality and lived in the pratimoksha and bodhisattva vows, purely practicing patience and perseverance, and undergoing great hardships in order to become enlightened and benefit sentient beings such as ourselves. As it says in the *Guru Puja*, the perfection of perseverance means willingly remaining for countless eons in the hottest hell for even one sentient being. This is how the Buddha practiced, without discouragement or depression, with great joy.

2. The Perseverance of Gathering Virtue

The second type of perseverance is the perseverance of gathering virtue, which means finding joy in practicing the Dharma. As is said in the *Compendium of the Perfections*:

If you have great perseverance completely free from discouragement, there is nothing that you cannot accomplish or attain.[65]

When we have perseverance to practice the Dharma, our life, whether long or short, becomes highly meaningful. How quickly we attain enlightenment depends on how much perseverance we have, because perseverance is the quality that keeps us from the distractions of worldly affairs, from laziness and sleep. The *Sagaramati-Requested Sutra* says,

> The lazy person has no generosity, and so forth up to wisdom.
> The lazy person cannot benefit others. The lazy person is far from
>   enlightenment.[66]

Unless we develop our perseverance, we will find it very difficult not to succumb to laziness, losing all the merit we have accumulated through falling into nonvirtue. When this happens, we won't even be able to achieve temporal success, let alone fulfill our ultimate purpose.

3. *The Perseverance of Working for the Welfare of Others*

Bodhisattvas work solely for the welfare of others and find incredible joy in doing so. This is the third kind of perseverance. No matter how long it takes and no matter how little progress we seem to make in helping others, we should never become discouraged. The *Guru Puja* says,

> Even if I must remain for an ocean of eons in the fiery hells
>   of Avici
> for the sake of even just one sentient being,
> I seek your blessings to complete the perfection of enthusiasm,
> that out of compassion untiringly strives for supreme
>   enlightenment.[67]

This verse shows us what the perfection of perseverance is, that for the sake of even one single sentient being we are able to work without discouragement or disillusionment, inexhaustibly, even if we have to endure the suffering of the lowest of the eight hot hells[68] for an ocean of eons for that sentient being. This is the hottest of the hot hells, where the body is completely one with the intense fire, and the only way a being is recognizable as sentient is by the screams; we suffer this for an uncountable number of eons, said to be more than there are drops of water in the Pacific Ocean. We need this kind of resolve.

In the *Adornment of the Mahayana Sutras*, Maitreya Buddha said,

> In order to generate a virtuous thought
> in the mind of one sentient being,
> a brave-hearted bodhisattva is happy even if they have to bear hardships
> without discouragement for a hundred eons.[69]

We have made each sentient being endure unimaginable suffering when they were our parent, not just as a human but as every type of being. They were obliged to create negative karma that caused them to be born in the lower realms and experience the most terrible suffering for eons. For us to bear hardships for a hundred eons is nothing compared with that. When we see this, for that one sentient being we gladly bear pain, sickness, hunger, thirst, heat, cold, and so forth, in order to help that being overcome their suffering and lead them into happiness.

Liberation is so attractive to us because it means the complete cessation of all samsaric suffering and its causes. It means we never have to worry about pain and problems, about getting cancer or being poor. How happy we would be if we could actually achieve this. And yet the bodhisattvas pray for just the opposite. To be able to experience such problems for the sake of all sentient beings is incredible bliss for them. This can only happen with bodhichitta—when a bodhisattva takes on the sole responsibility to free all sentient beings from all suffering. Whatever suffering the bodhisattva has to endure is nothing; they experience it joyfully.

How to Develop Perseverance

Great strength of will is needed even for worldly ends. Dictators have incredible determination and focus as they plot to invade and conquer other countries. Even if it takes them their entire lives, they realize their desire to destroy the other countries' defenses and take them over, using every resource they have. Hitler, for example, was a person of great determination. Look at the great destruction he caused to the countries in Europe. He could not have done this if he thought it was all too big for him to accomplish.

If strong, sustained energy is necessary for worldly pursuits, then there is no question it is needed for practicing the Dharma. We need the determination that we will work tirelessly, no matter how long it takes. If we do have such a resolve, we won't have to wait a hundred thousand eons. There are various methods that will free us from samsara very quickly, in three lifetimes or even in one. It depends on us putting sustained and strong energy into destroying our delusions, which is why the perfection of perseverance is so important.

Developing perseverance means overcoming the various forms of laziness, which are generally listed as three:

1. The laziness of procrastination
2. The laziness of being attached to worldly affairs
3. The laziness of discouragement and low self-worth

Of this Shantideva said,

> What are the adversaries of fortitude?
> They are: indolence, a fondness for evil, despondency, and
>   self-deprecation.[70]

In addition, there are qualities we need to develop, which the texts usually list as these:

- aspiration
- unwavering resolve

- joy
- correct application

1. Overcoming the Laziness of Procrastination

When I was studying for my US passport, I had to learn about American history, about how the US freed itself from British control and about how people fought for the end of slavery. I'm afraid I made a complete mess of it, getting Pearl Harbor confused with the Civil War and not knowing what the Stars and Stripes was. One person who struck me as amazing was Martin Luther King Jr., who worked so hard for the rights of black people in the US. But as difficult were the fights to end slavery, for equal rights, and for women's liberation, none of them are anywhere near as difficult or as urgent as the fight to be free from the dictatorship of the self-cherishing mind.

Under the yoke of the dictator—our self-cherishing—and controlled by his generals—the three poisons—we are fighting for our freedom. We must escape, and so we must use every means at our disposal. Because at present we have this perfect human rebirth, it is vital we don't waste a moment of it; we must use every moment to develop bodhichitta. And yet we find it so hard to even pick up a Dharma book!

Under the dictatorship of the self-cherishing mind, we have made ourselves slaves to its derivatives: ignorance, attachment, and anger, and the other disturbing emotions. From beginningless lives we have been under their control, completely misunderstanding what freedom is. We have mistakenly thought they were a means for gaining freedom, and so we have followed them and enslaved ourselves to them. We cry out, "I want to be myself!" and yet we follow our self-cherishing as it leads us from one problem to the next. Our worries and fears are unending. As soon as one ends, the next begins. It's the same thing again and again, like always opening a new box and finding the same things inside: relationship problems, work problems, and on and on. We think we are giving ourselves freedom by following the ego, but actually we are just working for our delusions—we are slaves to their dictates. Whatever our delusions want, we give in to them. With this totally wrong understanding, we force ourselves to suffer in samsara, just as we have from beginningless time. We have no energy for anything other than working for our delusions. We might be very active but this is laziness.

As Shantideva said,

> Indolence develops when, out of inertia,
> or due to a taste for pleasure, or due to mental torpor,
> or because one craves for the comforts of a soft pillow,
> one is not sensitive to the sufferings of transmigration.[71]

At present we find it hard to find the time to meditate or study any Dharma. To even chant a mantra seems a chore. On the other hand, we have great energy for watching television or going to parties, or just staying in bed. When we understand how attachment to worldly pleasures, to the eight worldly dharmas,[72] is trapping us, we can learn how real happiness lies in virtue. *Then*, when we have joy in virtue, we can turn our life around from nonvirtue to virtue.

Later in the chapter Shantideva said,

> You have obtained this human condition,
> which is like a raft—cross then the river of suffering.
> You fool, this is no time for sleep,
> you will not find this craft easily again.[73]

The "raft" means this perfect human rebirth, the raft we use to cross the suffering of samsara and attain enlightenment. Because of its rarity and preciousness, and because it can be lost at any moment, while we have it we must not waste a moment; we must not sleep. That doesn't mean we don't sleep at all. By "sleep" Shantideva means letting our vigilance waver, lapsing back into nonvirtuous actions, and wasting this precious chance we now have.

Of course, if we are attached to our bed then maybe Shantideva does mean sleep in that way. Maybe in that case we should follow the example of the monks and nuns in the big Tibetan monasteries and nunneries who often get up at three or four o'clock in the morning and do their prayers before a full day of study, pujas, and debate that very often doesn't finish until very late at night. They survive on a few hours' sleep each day because their minds are so energized with virtue, unlike we worldly people who need half the day to recover from the nonvirtuous activities that take up the other half.

Each second of this perfect human rebirth is more precious than skies filled with wish-granting jewels. Using this perfect human rebirth, within one second we can attain the three great meanings: a better future rebirth, liberation, and enlightenment. It gives us the most precious jewel of bodhichitta, which means we can fulfill our full potential and become a buddha in order to best serve others. Even if we don't have a dollar to our name, even if we are not sure where tonight's meal will come from, we are richer than a person possessing billions of diamonds and mountains of gold or even skies of wish-granting jewels.[74]

We have this human body endowed with its eight freedoms and ten richnesses, and because of that we can use it as a boat to cross the ocean of samsara to the other side, to reach the end of suffering and its causes. We can use this boat to cease not just the gross defilements that block us from liberation from suffering but also the subtle defilements that block us from full enlightenment. Therefore, while we have this boat, we must use it.

In chapter 4 of *A Guide to the Bodhisattva's Way of Life*, the chapter on conscientiousness, Shantideva showed us how rare obtaining such a human rebirth is—as rare as a blind turtle putting its neck through a golden ring floating on the ocean when it surfaces once every hundred years. Unless we take this precious opportunity now, the Lord of Death will come and our work will never be completed.

I remember the second pilgrimage I made to Tibet. Very near the birthplace of Lama Yeshe we came across a truck filled with thornbushes with a calf stuffed in one corner. It had big, terrified eyes, and we all knew it was on its way to the butcher. Knowing this was the calf's fate, we stopped the driver and bought it.

When cows reach the slaughterhouse, as they are roughly pulled from the trucks by ropes through the rings in their noses and dragged to the slaughter yard, they pull back, instinctively fearing what will happen. The butcher then kills them with an axe or a big knife.

If they had human bodies, they could plead for their lives in billions of words; they could pay whatever bribe was demanded; they could do all sorts of things to escape. But they cannot communicate, and so, no matter how much fear they have, there is nothing they can do. They must wait to be slaughtered to become food for human beings.

They have all been human beings like us in numberless past lives but because they were unable to transform their minds by practicing the Dharma, they were forced to transmigrate into animal bodies and so suffer this result.

We have all sorts of karma, virtuous and nonvirtuous, on our mental continuum, collected since beginningless time. If we check to see how much of each kind of karma we accumulate in one day, can we truthfully say there is more virtuous than nonvirtuous? What actions, no matter how small, were done with the attachment clinging to this life? What actions were done with a bodhichitta motivation? Or with the right view or renunciation? What was the motivation for eating our breakfast? If it was attachment to this life, then each bite was nonvirtue, the cause of suffering; if it was renunciation, right view, or bodhichitta, then each bite was virtue, the cause of happiness. In the same way, when we check the motivation for going to work, for shopping, for sleeping—for all the many actions we do in one day—we can see if we are creating more virtuous or more nonvirtuous karma.

This is the choice we face every second of our life. Whatever we do can be virtuous or nonvirtuous, it can be Dharma or non-Dharma, it can be the cause for future happiness or future suffering. And so whatever we do can lead us to the fortunate upper realms or to the utter misery of the lower realms. This is why we must be so mindful of everything we do. If we are not careful with all our actions of body, speech, and mind, then the habitual nonvirtuous minds can take over, and we can do things that harm ourselves and others and plant the seeds for countless rebirths in the lower realms.

Reflecting on Impermanence Generates Perseverance

In one of the sutras it says that when a king dies, he leaves behind his palaces, his wealth, his wives, and his luxury; when a beggar dies, he leaves behind his walking stick. No matter how different their lifestyles were, they are both completely equal in death in what they can take with them—nothing. Like pulling a hair from butter, where not one atom of butter comes with the hair, at death our mind leaves our body and all our possessions and takes another body. The only thing we take with us is our accumulation of karmic imprints, both positive and negative.

When we die with attachment, we are terrified of losing everything, suddenly seeing all these things we have clung to being taken from us. In this state, we leave this life and go to the next. There is a popular saying:

> You cannot be sure which will come first,
> Tomorrow or the next life,
> Therefore, do not put effort into tomorrow's plans
> But instead it is worthwhile to attend to the next life.[75]

We leave everything behind when we die, even our body, this thing we cherish above all else. At present we treasure our friends, seeing them as sources of our happiness, but when we die they can do nothing to help us. They cannot share our suffering in the slightest. Furthermore, our attachment to them becomes a huge hindrance to our peaceful death. And so even if we have been with them all our life, at death they become capable of bringing us great harm.

Nothing is definite in samsara. As the Buddha said,

> Everything together falls apart;
> everything rising up collapses;
> every meeting ends in parting;
> every life ends in death.[76]

There is the story of the four people who craved four different things. There was the king who craved power, the trader who craved possessions, the person who craved friends, and the person who craved a long life. The king was unable to hold on to his power and became powerless and miserable; the trader lost every possession; the person who craved friends was completely separated from them; and the person who craved a long life died young. Whatever we cling to we are bound to lose.

When we see this, we realize that we should not postpone our Dharma practice. We might wake up one day thinking we will live for a long time—and we will be dead before that day finishes. Or perhaps we will still be alive tomorrow. Who knows? The only guarantee is that we will die. Without that certainty, will we have the strength to go against our habitual laziness?

The great yogi Milarepa is a wonderful example of perseverance. Through reflecting on impermanence and death he found the courage to withstand incredible hardships in order to practice the Dharma, including living in a cave with nothing but a cooking pot and nettles to eat. Later on, he was able to control the four elements, meaning nothing could affect his health, but in the beginning he had to overcome the sufferings of heat, cold, hunger, and great discomfort in order to meditate. He said,

> I fled to the mountains because I feared death.
> I have realized emptiness, the mind's primordial state.
> Were I to die now, I have no fear.[77]

Reflecting well on impermanence and death gives us the perseverance we need to withstand any hardship we encounter without fear. While we cling to samsara we fear so many things, but when we deeply understand the impermanence of all things, including our own life, we can overcome the cycle of death and rebirth. Rather than the sort of perseverance that makes us pursue what is meaningless, here, with the courage gained from the reflection on impermanence and death, we have the power and determination to overcome our delusions and only do what is meaningful in our life.

2. Overcoming the Laziness of Attachment to Samsaric Activities

The next sort of laziness we must overcome is the laziness of being attached to worldly affairs. Laziness, in this context, is not what we would usually associate with the word. We can enjoy chasing worldly pleasures and work hard in order to have what we want—we can be incredibly busy—but that is considered laziness because it distracts us from our Dharma practice. It is the love of nonvirtuous acts and the reluctance to do virtuous ones.

Perhaps at present getting up to meditate still requires an effort. Because our bed is comfortable and the weather is cold, we stay in bed until the last minute, rush breakfast, and hurry off to work. We feel we have no time to meditate, but that is a misconception; there is time to meditate if we make the time. Time is not inherently existent; it ceases and arises, and we can create the causes and conditions for more time to meditate if we really want to. At present, comfort and breakfast seem more important than meditating, but if we could understand the importance of our Dharma practice, there would be plenty of time.

While we still need to sleep, even if we are making the most of this perfect human rebirth, it is definitely possible to get by on less sleep in order to do more meditation. It might be difficult at present but, as Shantideva said, everything becomes easier with familiarization. We can get into the habit of rising a half hour or an hour earlier in order to meditate.

We have energy for whatever we have an interest in. We have no problem working hard at things such as planning our holiday, because they are important to us. Whether we have time for practice—to do meditation or recite prayers—is a question of interest, of how important we feel the Dharma is, how much we want to help other sentient beings, how much we understand about impermanence and death, the suffering of the lower realms, and so forth.

And yet now we delay and procrastinate because we think that practicing the Dharma might be too hard or require too much effort. Overcoming laziness, being reluctant to do something, is just a matter of understanding its importance. When we see the Dharma as even more important than worldly activities, we will have the energy and perseverance to speedily progress on the path.

3. Overcoming the Laziness of Discouragement

The last of the three sorts of laziness, the laziness of discouragement and low self-worth, can be overcome by understanding how practicing the Dharma is the infallible cure for all our problems. With physical illnesses such as cancer, although medicine might cure them, there is no guarantee they will never recur. The Dharma is the medicine that cures the delusions, and once we have eliminated all our delusions it is impossible to ever experience them again.

Seeing there is the chance to finally completely remove even the seed of delusions, no matter how long it takes, should give us great determination to practice as purely as we can and not be discouraged when difficulties arise. When we find it hard to protect our karma and not commit nonvirtuous actions, instead of becoming discouraged, we should think about how long we have been sick in samsara because of these countless delusions, and how, once we have destroyed them, they can never return. This will strengthen our will and make us even more determined to persevere in our Dharma practice.

Overcoming our delusions is not easy. Making a rocket and landing it on the moon is difficult, but controlling and overcoming our delusions is far more difficult. It is also far more beneficial and valuable. For one thing, we don't need to purify our delusions to land a rocket on the moon—we can do that while we are full of delusions—whereas to even enter the Mahayana at the first path requires incredible purification.

Once we have completely purified all obscurations and accumulated all the merit and have become fully enlightened, we will have completed our Dharma practice. There is no higher goal than this. Therefore we should not have a small heart when we are practicing the Dharma—we should not be scared away by physical and mental difficulties that arise in our path.

Say, for instance, we are planning to climb Mount Everest. Despite knowing the extreme difficulty of the climb and the great dangers of the route to the top, our desire to reach the summit is so strong we have no doubt we can overcome all obstacles. And when we are on the trek, no matter what occurs—the snow, the wind, the avalanches, the physical hardships, the altitude sickness, and so forth—our determination to reach the top allows us to carry on where other people would have turned back. With this iron-clad determination we will certainly reach the peak. However, if we thought it was going to be a safe and easy trek, then with the first avalanche we would become completely discouraged and give up the whole expedition.

This is the same with our Dharma practice. We should not expect to overcome all our gross delusions after a few months' meditation. If we expect quick results, we can become easily disillusioned. Having unrealistic expectations will bring problems, causing our development to be up and down, and maybe even causing us to abandon our practice altogether.

We need to be farsighted. Our goal has to stretch further than bubble gum being pulled from the mouth! Unless we have patience with ourselves and perseverance to continue when there are hardships, our mind will waver whenever we encounter a problem. Even the buddhas cannot count the number of delusions we have on our mindstream, so we shouldn't be disillusioned when we don't gain realizations in a few weeks. We must have the energy to persevere for a long time, working continuously to destroy our delusions, thinking that even if it takes a hundred thousand eons we will never be discouraged.

Overcoming Self-Contempt

When problems occur, we can easily become discouraged and feel that we are hopeless, that there is no way we can practice the Dharma. "I'm ignorant, I'm terrible, I can't do anything." "I have so much anger, I can never get rid of it." "I'm supposed to be renouncing attachment, but I'm just getting more attached to things." "Dharma is too difficult for me to understand. It takes too long and I have no patience." This kind of thinking can be very damaging. The mind cannot be transformed instantaneously. That's the American style, where everybody is so busy and everything gets done so quickly. Dharma is training the mind, and that takes time. However, that busy energy that people have in the West is extremely good if it can be used to practice the Dharma. Keeping busy in the Dharma is excellent.

When we are discouraged and feeling strong self-contempt, we should remember this advice: "When the discouraged mind arises, elevate the thought." When we feel our spirit is low, right down on the ground, we should lift it up by thinking about what we have and realizing how extremely fortunate we are. When we look at our perfect human rebirth, with its eight freedoms and ten richnesses, we can see our huge potential. We are not worthless at all but can succeed in whatever we want to do. This technique is extremely useful when we are feeling discouraged about our Dharma practice, but we can even use it for worldly things such as when we feel we are failing in our business or in a relationship.

Of course it is difficult to change bad habits. Our entire life and for countless lives before we have been under the control of attachment. We cannot expect that to drastically change in a few weeks or months or even years. Even habits such as smoking are extremely difficult to break. We should therefore not feel discouraged when we fail to see any progress after some time. Such discouragement could make us give up—we might think that the Dharma doesn't work and return to our old life and our old problems.

Although Milarepa attained enlightenment in one lifetime, he had developed his understanding of emptiness and his renunciation in previous lifetimes. Guru Shakyamuni Buddha also developed his merit over eons. To expect instant realizations is a fantasy. How can that happen? This is the expectation of a limited mind.

We can only purify our negativities and create merit little by little, drop by drop. When we see this, we can develop the determination to persevere no matter how hard it is. Then, whether we are up or down, we see the importance of perseverance. Shantideva said,

How could he be discouraged,
this sage who moves in this way from bliss to bliss?
I have obtained this chariot of the thought of awakening,
which leaves behind all weariness and fatigue.[78]

Gathering the Favorable Conditions

As well as overcoming the three forms of laziness, we need to gather the favorable conditions for generating perseverance.

Aspiration

Because in the past we did not understand karma and therefore created nonvirtue, we must now face suffering. If we had only practiced the Dharma in the past, then this would not have happened. Understanding this deeply gives us the aspiration to only practice the Dharma. Of this, Shantideva said,

> I lacked in past lives the will to practice Dharma,
> therefore now I have been born into such a miserable birth.
> Seeing this, who would abandon
> his determination to practice Dharma.
>
> The Sage has said that zeal is the root of all virtue;
> and the root of this zeal
> is the constant contemplation
> of the eventual fruit of the ripening of our actions.[79]

Our happiness depends on our attitude and our actions, on whether every action of body, speech, and mind is one of virtue or nonvirtue. With a bodhichitta motivation, every action will not only be the remedy to cut the root of suffering; it will also be the cause for happiness, to liberate ourselves from samsara and to attain full enlightenment. Living our life with this motivation is the best way to spend every moment— it's the best preparation for death and the best preparation for all the coming future lives. Each time we transform our mind into renuncia-tion, bodhichitta, and right view, we are preparing our mind. This is something we must persevere with. Shantideva said,

> Therefore, I should exercise my will in meritorious
>   activities,
> having cultivated it zealously in this way.
> One should cultivate it by adopting pride
> as it is recommended in the Vajradhvaja.

> First one should consider the circumstances,
> and then decide whether to go ahead or not.
> For it is better not to begin at all,
> than to begin and then give up.

> The habit will persist in future lives too,
> and the suffering resulting from sin will increase.
> Another worthy enterprise will be neglected, time and
>   effort will be lost,
> and you will have not accomplished the task you had
>   begun.[80]

Once we have begun to transform our mind we must continue. If we become discouraged, we will return to old habits and this will increase in future lives, causing even more suffering. We must see how the source of all the happiness and success of our future lives depends on how much we are able to develop our mind by practicing Dharma now. Whether it is going to be easy or difficult, whether we will be able to have another human rebirth or not, depends on how we live each day, how much we can develop our mind now. We have this responsibility to our next life.

Unwavering Resolve

Along with aspiration, we need unwavering resolve or steadfastness in order to never falter in our efforts to transform our mind. Of this Shantideva said,

> As one would pick up his sword with great fear,
> if it was dropped in the midst of battle,
> so, if one loses the sword of mindfulness,
> one will pick it up at once fearing the hells.

> As poison, once it enters the bloodstream
> will spread throughout the body,
> a vice that finds a weak spot
> will spread through the mind.

> One who has adopted the vows should be like the man
> who was forced to carry a bowl filled to the rim with oil under
>   threat of death if he spilled any.
> As he was watched by sword-bearing guards,
> he could think of nothing but that bowl, for fear of stumbling
>   and dying.

> Therefore, if one feels stupor and sloth approaching,
> one should react swiftly against them,
> as anyone would jump up
> if a snake fell on his lap.[81]

Here is vital advice on how to practice awareness during our meditation session and in our daily life. Because our delusions can arise at any moment, overwhelming us and causing us to create nonvirtue, we must therefore always be on the lookout, constantly protecting our mind. If we ever become aware of a nonvirtuous thought arising, we should shake it off like we would shake off a snake we found in our lap when we woke from a deep sleep, not hesitating for one instant for fear of being bitten.

Each time there is some unwholesome thought or action, we should see its damage, regret having done it, and analyze why it happened, resolving never to do it again. Seeing the importance of Dharma practice, we should not allow anything to interfere with us developing our mind, either laziness or attachment to worldly things. We should not be caught in the comfort of this life.

Whereas worldly beings cherish comfort and happiness and have feelings for those who help them but not those who harm them, we should reverse those attitudes. Geshe Chen Ngawa advised Dharma practitioners to have these four attitudes:

- to cherish sentient beings more than buddhas
- to cherish suffering more than happiness
- to cherish enemies more than friends
- to cherish others more than ourselves

This is the unwavering resolve we should have, but it seems the opposite of Western psychology, which says we should concentrate on self-interest rather than thinking about others. Cherishing ourselves is healthy, whereas renouncing ourselves is unhealthy.

I remember a student in London a long time ago being very puzzled by this. He had read in important books on Western psychology that happiness comes from things we do, whereas problems come from what others do to us, and therefore we are right to blame other people, such as our parents, for our unhappiness. This view is missing an understanding of karma. When we understand karma we can see that everything comes from the mind and that we are responsible for our own happiness and suffering. Only by renouncing our self-cherishing can we be free from suffering, and that means renouncing our attachment and our view of the person who harms our self-cherishing as being our enemy. Another thing missing from that view is compassion—seeing the suffering of others as unbearable and wishing to do something about it. Basically, because karma was missing, compassion was missing.

When we only think of short-term happiness for ourselves, we are bound to only create the cause of suffering for ourselves. When we think of long-term happiness for others, we create the cause of happiness for both ourselves and others. I remember I suggested that after that student had attained his degree in philosophy, he should discard those Western psychology books and use his own wisdom.

Rejoicing

The practice of rejoicing in merit is a very important practice we should do as often as possible. Among the virtues, it is the best one to practice because it is the easiest. It is simply a mental action—one that accumulates merit as infinite as space. Rejoicing increases any merit we have created, like investing a hundred dollars and getting interest all the time until we have thousands, tens of thousands, hundreds of thousands, then millions of dollars.

When we rejoice in the merit we created, we accumulate more merit than we did when we actually performed the action. When we rejoice in the merit of other sentient beings, if their level of mind is lower than ours we accumulate double the merit they do, whereas if their level of mind is higher than ours we accumulate half that merit. For instance, if we rejoice in the merit that a bodhisattva creates in one day, we accumulate half that merit, which would otherwise take us at least fifteen thousand years to accumulate.

Most of the time, we see happiness as experiencing sense pleasures, so we use this precious human rebirth to create causes of suffering. When somebody gives us a cup of tea or an ice cream or we make a dollar's profit in our business, we feel so happy. When we fail to get such things, we feel miserable. Because we feel competitive with others, we are jealous and unhappy when they succeed and we don't. This is how we lead our life.

When we learn to appreciate our precious human existence, however, we learn that these things are unimportant. Our joy will come from creating virtue. We could miss out on a cup of tea or even lose all our money without any sense of unhappiness. Only creating virtue matters, and when we do, we have good reason to rejoice.

Correct Application

If our body and mind become tired through having exerted much energy or if there is a danger that tiredness will make us unable to continue in the future, it is necessary to take a short rest. On recovery, we can resume our practice of perseverance. As Shantideva said,

> If one is not suited to the task,
> the moment one realizes this one should abandon it.
> And once a task has been completed,
> one should give it up for the one that will follow.[82]

DEVELOPING THE POWER OF PERSEVERANCE

We need an extensive mind, one that sustains the determination to achieve what we wish, no matter what obstacle we encounter: illness, heat, cold, or whatever. We cannot succeed with a weak mind. Just as Milarepa bore great hardships to gain realizations, living an austere life and eating only nettles, we need continued, strong practice.

It is a great mistake to say a prayer such as the *Foundation of All Good Qualities* with palms together and eyes squeezed shut, wishing to generate this realization immediately and then, at the end of the prayer, feel disappointed we have not succeeded. Realizations will not happen until we have overcome obstacles; we must have the determination to face them and destroy them.

There are said to be three attitudes needed when meditating on the lamrim:

- generating a long view
- generating an extensive thought
- being relaxed

Always having a long view means always having the motivation to achieve enlightenment. Having an extensive thought means determining to progress through the graduated paths of the three capable beings in order to do that. Even though the body of our actual practice is bodhichitta, the graduated path of the higher capable being, we need to encompass the other two paths as well, never forgetting the preliminary meditations that will enable us to attain bodhichitta. We need the extensive thought that no matter how long it takes, we will persevere until we succeed.

The third attitude is having a relaxed mind. It's important not to squeeze our mind—that is, to hold it tight for a few weeks and then, unable to sustain that, completely lose our meditation. After that, because nothing has happened, there is no energy to continue. Then we are *completely* relaxed, which is not the meaning of this third attitude! Rather than a short, too-intense time of meditation that is followed by collapse, with the mind slack and unable to focus at all, we should maintain a relaxed balance, neither too tight nor too loose. In that way we can sustain our practice.

It is unwise to rush to the mountains for an intense retreat after being inspired by teachings from the guru, only to burn out after a few days and develop complete aversion for the practice because of it. We have to be sensible and do the practice that is most appropriate for us at this moment.

Making the Mind Serviceable
In the *Bodhisattva's Jewel Garland*, Atisha said,

> Discard all lingering doubts
> And strive with dedication in your practice.
> Thoroughly relinquish sloth, mental dullness, and laziness,
> And strive always with joyful perseverance.
>
> With mindfulness, awareness, and heedfulness,
> Constantly guard the gateways of your senses.
> Again and again, three times both day and night,
> Examine the flow of your thoughts.[83]

This is essential advice for developing our mind in bodhichitta. Having certainty in the worthiness of the Dharma, we should always exert ourselves, persevering no matter what problems we encounter. When we try to meditate, we need to overcome sleepiness, dullness, and laziness. Furthermore, we should always try to be joyful.

When we study any lamrim subject in enough depth we can see its value, and this gives us courage to continue. We can keep our mind in virtue every day by remembering that the sufferings of the lower realms are the results of negative karma such as the ten nonvirtues. Nagarjuna compared this to a rider keeping their horse on the right track by whipping its flanks. When the mind is still apt to wander into nonvirtue, we need to whip it back into the virtuous path by remembering the lower realms.

Then, seeing how the whole of samsara is suffering, we are inspired to do whatever we need in order to become free from it. For that, we happily take the various levels of vows: the pratimoksha vows, the bodhisattva vows, and the tantric vows. Then, seeing how all other sentient beings are suffering so much, strong compassion naturally arises and, with the wish to help them in whatever way we can, we do everything possible to attain bodhichitta and full enlightenment. This gives us the perseverance to never waver from our Dharma practice.

For this, we always practice awareness and conscientiousness in order to protect the doors of our senses. This is like the example from Shantideva above: somebody carrying a bowl full of mustard oil would be incredibly attentive if threatened with death should one drop be spilled. It is that important to keep our mind alert so that we don't slip into nonvirtue. Our awareness of the consequences of creating negative karma—the unbearable suffering of the lower realms—is like the person holding the sword.

By maintaining our remembrance and awareness we can have conscientiousness. We will always keep our mind on the path with guru devotion, renunciation, bodhichitta, and right view, and if we have a tantric practice, we will keep it purely.

The perfect meditation needs two elements: remembrance and aware-ness. Awareness is being able to recognize when our mind is distracted, when it is not in the Dharma. Remembrance is holding the mind on that virtuous object, always remembering it. If our mind slips and we lose the object, not remembering it, and if we don't have the awareness that we have slipped, we can waste many hours distracted with nonvir-tuous objects.

We must always protect the doors of our senses from any object that might cause attachment, anger, or any other negative emotion to arise. This can only happen if we watch our mind day and night, practicing mindfulness, checking whether our mind is Dharma or non-Dharma, whether it is virtuous or nonvirtuous. This is a huge job and it needs great perseverance.

5 : CONCENTRATION

THE FIFTH PERFECTION is the perfection of concentration, which is *dhyana* in Sanskrit and *samten* in Tibetan. On the path to enlightenment, this is seen as calm abiding conjoined with the penetrative insight that is the wisdom of understanding emptiness.

Calm abiding, which is *shamatha* in Sanskrit or *shiné* in Tibetan, refers to the ability to abide steadily on an object of meditation for an extended period of time without any distractions.

Single-pointed concentration, which is *samadhi* in Sanskrit or *tingédzin* in Tibetan, refers to the deep meditative absorption free from discursive thought. There are two types of meditation: single-pointed or fixed meditation, and analytical meditation. Except for single-pointed meditation, all the other meditations we do within the lamrim—meditations on our precious human rebirth, bodhichitta, and so forth—are analytical, where we analyze the subject through logic and scriptural sources.

Within analytical meditation, however, there should also be single-pointed meditation. For instance, say we are meditating on the perfect human rebirth and at the end of the analysis the thought strongly arises of how incredibly precious this life is. If that happens, we should place our mind on that feeling as long as we can. Holding the mind on that experience means that the next time we meditate on that subject it will be stronger and there will be a greater possibility of actually attaining a realization.

To avert and then destroy our delusions, we need to study what the Buddha taught about them. Analytical and fixed meditations together give us the power and focus to really investigate as well as the understanding to take our analysis to its most profound level. There is no need for faith or anything else at all; it is pure rational analysis, and yet, used in the right way, it can lead us all the way to enlightenment. This is unbelievable! This is mind-blowing!

We realize emptiness by conjoining a calm-abiding meditation with a deep analysis of emptiness, called "special insight" or *vipashyana*, in Tibetan, *lhaktong*. The texts explain that we first have a realization of calm abiding; we are able to concentrate single-pointedly, totally free from attachment–scattering thought, which is *göpa* in Tibetan, and sinking thought or dullness, which is *jingwa* in Tibetan. Only when we are totally free from these subtle obstacles can we concentrate single-pointedly.

I use the term *attachment–scattering thought* to differentiate it from just scattering thought, which is *towa* in Tibetan. When we are focused on an object of meditation and our mind wanders to another object— either a nonvirtuous one, such as the desire for food, or even a virtuous one, such as thinking of the Buddha—that is towa. When the mind stays in meditation but moves from the object we should be concentrating on to another object of meditation, such as from a visualization of Tara[84] to another deity, then that is göpa. Although it might still be a strong, focused meditation, it is considered attachment–scattering thought and an obstacle to our meditation.

We all have scattering and sinking thoughts when we try to meditate, but these distractions are very gross compared with the very subtle ones we must overcome to attain shamatha. Currently, under the control of attachment and other disturbing thoughts, concentration is impossible. It's like our mind is fragmented, like a rock that has been shattered into tiny shards, or like chopped meat. We are unable to visualize clearly, maybe not even able to recite the opening prayers properly. Doing a visualization becomes like trying to cross over a huge mountain; no matter how hard we work, it is incredibly difficult. This can easily cause us to become tense and lead to *lung*, wind disease, which can bring physical pain in our heart, paranoia, and even insanity.

The texts talk of various levels of subtlety of sinking and scattering thoughts. The gross sinking mind is also called the foggy mind, *mukpa*, in Tibetan. It refers to a mind that has no clarity at all, like dark, foggy weather. Our mind is sluggish and sleepy, and often we do actually fall asleep. With the sinking thought, on the other hand, we can hold the object but not clearly, and with the subtle sinking thought we can hold the object clearly—very clearly—but the way of apprehending the object is weak; there is no energy. Because of this lack of intensity, this is considered an imperfect meditation.

There are eight remedies[85] we use to overcome these obstacles, gradually moving through the nine levels of concentration until we achieve calm abiding. We will only be completely free from attachment–scattering thought and sinking thought upon reaching the ninth level of calm abiding.

Within an experience of calm abiding we can generate a realization of emptiness from the analytical meditations on emptiness we have done, which induces an ecstasy of body and mind. This whole experience is what is called the union of calm abiding and special insight.

Through developing concentration, we can attain great powers. As we progress through the nine levels of concentration, we experience greater and greater degrees of bliss, free from all distraction and sinking thought. However, that is not the ultimate reason for developing single-pointed concentration. We need to use that concentration to have the power to penetrate the subjects of the lamrim and especially the ultimate nature of reality. As it gets more familiar with the path, our mind actually becomes the path.

At present, our concentration is incredibly weak and our understanding is incredibly shallow. Any subject we study is blurred by lack of insight and warped by our deluded thinking, and when we try to meditate on it, our meditation can rarely go to any depth because of our lack of concentration. But this will change. Our progress will probably not be quick, but it will be definite if we keep at it. For now, we will slip off the object of our meditation and spend many wasted hours dreaming rather than meditating, but we will improve, finally getting to the stage where we can concentrate for hours without distraction.

Even now, we can use awareness, introspection, to check whether our mind is concentrated or not. In meditation or even just in our daily activities, we can keep a small part of our mind as a spy, checking what emotions are arising and why, checking how we are using our mind and whether what we are doing is beneficial.

CONCENTRATION ALONE IS NOT ENOUGH

Many traditions have a practice of concentration; it is not just a Buddhist teaching. For instance, the Hindu religion places great emphasis on samadhi meditations, and there are many practitioners who are able to gain the realization of samadhi through them. However, just having control of the mind—being able to focus on an object without sluggishness or distraction—is not the penetrative insight or vipashyana that realizes the true nature of things.

Concentration is not specifically a practice of a higher capable being. Even with the middle capable being, the three higher trainings needed to free ourselves from samsara are morality, concentration, and wisdom. In the lamrim texts such as *Lamrim Chenmo*, however, the six perfections, including concentration,[86] come after bodhichitta. The perfection of concentration becomes the cause for enlightenment when we practice calm abiding using emptiness as the object and bodhichitta as the basis. It can never become the cause of suffering.

With just the three higher trainings we could enter the Hinayana path, the path of individual liberation, and achieve freedom from samsara for ourselves, without focusing our efforts on the well-being of all others. When that happens, our mind sort of dissolves, like becoming intoxicated, and it remains concentrated on that sphere of peace and happiness for an incredibly long period, for many eons.

Arhats who have attained this everlasting happiness of self-liberation do not have the same degree of compassion for all sentient beings that bodhisattvas do. They do not have the sense of responsibility to help all sentient beings be free from suffering, to take the entire responsibility on themselves. Instead, they stay in that incredibly blissful state for millions of eons, unable to benefit other beings, until a buddha finally awakens them by giving them special signs and calling them to follow the Mahayana path in order to attain full enlightenment. The main aim of Mahayana is not to attain enlightenment but to free all other beings from all suffering, which is why we need to be enlightened and to develop all the skills that are needed for that. *That* is why we need shamatha and an understanding of emptiness, and why concentration comes after bodhichitta in the lamrim texts.

To attain calm abiding, we need many other factors such as perseverance, the fourth perfection. The mind of calm abiding does not come from its own side; we need to do a lot of hard work to get there. Without renouncing attachment to this life, without bearing the hardships needed to develop on the path to enlightenment, how can we hope to attain perfect concentration? To put a lot of effort into developing concentration for a little while, stop, and then try again some time later will not work. Only through perseverance can we hope to attain our goal.

We also need morality. Until we have perfect morality there will be disturbances that will block perfect concentration. In his *Middle Length Lamrim*,[87] Lama Tsongkhapa used the analogy of studying a beautiful drawing on a wall using a butter lamp. The lamp needs to be not only bright but also unmoved by any wind. No matter how bright, a flickering light will not reveal the painting to us. Similarly, the wind of our delusions will cause the flame of concentration to flicker, to be unstable. When we have calmed our delusions, the flame of concentration can shine with complete stability, perfectly revealing the object of our meditation. This cannot happen while the mind is agitated due to lack of morality, distracted by sense objects.

When we hear about the nine levels of concentration and what they entail, moving through them might seem an impossible task, but we can definitely attain calm abiding if we have the base of morality. Then, as Lama Tsongkhapa said, we will be able to hold the mind as stable and firm as a mountain for as long as we want, without the slightest distraction. This is a very worthwhile goal.

Because intense concentration is impossible while the mind is clouded by delusions, we also need strong purification practices. There are many very logical, profound subjects in Buddhism we are currently unable to understand because of our obscured mind, but with purification our mind will become more focused and our understanding clearer. Many subjects that cannot even be imagined at present will become clear as we purify the mind. This requires time, patience, and perseverance.

For instance, of the six realms[88] Buddhism talks about, because we can see the animal realm we accept the teachings on it, but the teachings on the hungry ghosts and the hell beings are more difficult to accept. We cannot see these realms and, because our understanding is limited, we probably currently find such teachings on them hard to believe. When our mind is sufficiently purified, we will be able to not only understand what these realms are but we will also be able to see them without the need to physically go to such places.

The reason we meditate on topics such as the lower realms now is to prepare our mind for when we can actually apprehend these things. We get a feeling for such topics and that makes our later meditations much more effective. Because their minds were completely purified of all duality, Guru Shakyamuni Buddha and the later great teachers gave explanations that came from their own experience. We cannot contradict them simply because we ourselves have not experienced such things.

In the lamrim, most of the meditations that come before shamatha are analytical. We can only gain realizations of the different lamrim topics by thoroughly investigating them in meditation. For instance, when we study the explanations of impermanence in the texts, we go from instinctively feeling that things are permanent to beginning to doubt that they are. Then, with further checking, their impermanence becomes a certainty. Without relying on analytical meditations, we cannot break our instinctive mistaken belief in permanence. Checking on the validity of the logical reasonings in the Dharma texts is so important. If we are going to transform our life through accepting these teachings as true, we need to discover their validity through our own analysis.

This is true even of worldly people doing worldly activities. Whenever we buy something, we first investigate it to see that it is worth it. Where it was made, what materials are used, how reliable it is—there are many considerations we carefully weigh before we renounce our money. And we make sure we renounce as little money as possible for the best possible product! We even do this for something that only lasts a day or two, such as vegetables, so why not for the lamrim topics in the Dharma? It is extremely foolish to blindly accept a philosophy we will use for our entire life without checking it thoroughly.

For instance, say that we are cheated in a business transaction. Somebody sells us a faulty product and we lose all our money because of it. That in itself does not cause us to create negative karma or bind us to wrong conceptions. On the other hand, when we don't check which meditations are beneficial, we can meditate on an object that habituates us to wrong thinking, locking us into our ignorance. Then each time we meditate, rather than developing wisdom through our meditation, we close the door to wisdom and develop ignorance instead.

There are also many people who believe that any thought appearing during meditation is a distraction and a hindrance, and therefore analytical meditation is not really meditation. They think meditation means clearing the mind completely. Such a meditation on nothingness can never solve any problems; it can never stop suffering.

Concentration without Peace

We should also understand that when we develop strong concentration, we don't necessarily automatically overcome our delusions. People who can concentrate for extended periods can still fight, argue, and abuse others and feel negative emotions such as greed, hatred, and pride.

It is said, "The unpeaceful mind can arise by meditating on the concentration of mental quietude." Generally, meditating is supposed to give rise to a mind of peace, so what does the "unpeaceful mind" mean in this context? Mental quietude, shamatha, just means the quiet mind, free from sinking or scattering thoughts. To have such a mind does not mean we have freed ourselves from nonvirtuous thoughts. Like having a field of potatoes where the weeds have not been pulled out, if we try to do a shamatha meditation without uprooting the weeds of our delusions, thoughts of greed, anger, pride, and the like can still arise.

For example, despite going to a spot high in the mountains and spending years on shamatha meditations, we may still be plagued with problems of frustration, depression, partiality, and so forth, because of our root delusions.[89] Even in isolation, we could still be attached to the comforts of this life, such as possessions, reputation, and the like. The foundation is the self-cherishing mind, and until it is uprooted from our mind all the other weeds of delusions that grow from it will be there, interfering with the crops of virtue we are trying to grow.

The unpeaceful mind does not manifest during a shamatha meditation because our disturbed negative emotions have been temporarily calmed rather than eliminated. While we still have attachment to this life's comforts, however, negative minds will arise when we come out of meditation. Until we can remove the root of our delusions, it is extremely difficult to become a perfect meditator. In the second *Stages of Meditation* volume, the great Indian pandit Kamalashila said,

> Cultivating just shamatha alone does not get rid of a practitioner's obscurations; it only suppresses the afflictions for a while. Unless you have the light of wisdom, you do not destroy the dormant tendencies.[90]

On the other hand, when we have subdued our mind, even problems that arise in meditation can be used. It is said that with the subdued mind, even sickness, spirit harm, and human and nonhuman enemies become helpers. There are many techniques for transforming problems into the causes of happiness, where instead of letting them disturb us, we use them to help our Dharma practice.

The Ten Bhumis

Whether we work toward liberation or enlightenment, there are five stages we pass through called the five paths: the path of merit, the path of preparation, the path of seeing, the path of meditation, and the path of no more learning.

Within the Mahayana tradition, the first path, the *path of merit*, refers to the period when we work diligently accumulating merit—by listening to the Dharma, reflecting on the meaning, meditating, and so forth—in order to fully realize the teachings within the mindstream in the future. With the *path of preparation*, we gain greater insight into emptiness, but because we have yet to realize it directly, we are still an ordinary being. This is nonetheless a penetrative insight on emptiness, where the conceptual understanding of emptiness is conjoined with a very deep meditative experience.

Then, through the continual meditation on emptiness, our mind reaches the *path of seeing*, and we have a direct realization of emptiness. We become an arya being. We do not have to go through death again, and therefore we won't have to experience rebirth, old age, sickness, and yet another death.

At this level, we are on the first of the ten bodhisattva levels, or *bhumi* in Sanskrit, that we will slowly progress through until enlightenment on the fifth path. With this first level, we are able to manifest in a hundred forms; we are able to experience a hundred universes with our psychic powers; we are able to see a hundred eons into the past and future; we are able to attain a hundred concentrations and able to travel to a hundred buddha fields[91] in order to receive teachings from the buddhas there. With the hundred different bodies simultaneously manifesting, we are able to give teachings to sentient beings and ripen their minds. We abide in this state at this level for a hundred eons.

Only the first stage of the bodhisattva levels occurs on the third path. The others occur when we have reached the fourth path, the *path of meditation*. Here, our direct realization of emptiness becomes stabilized and continuous. On the second bodhisattva level, all the accomplishments we could do a hundredfold on the first level become a thousandfold, so we are able to transform into a thousand bodies, travel to a thousand buddha fields, and so forth. Then with each succeeding level this number multiplies, a thousand becoming hundreds of thousands, then millions up to unimaginable millions.

Even with the fourth path there are still very subtle residual defilements, and so during that time we work on destroying even these. When that happens, when we realize the tenth bodhisattva level, we enter the *path of no more learning*, which directly precedes the attainment of enlightenment.

Developing Concentration within a Retreat

What is the importance of doing a retreat?[92] It is not simply to be quiet, to have a break from your family and work. One simple reason is happiness. You do a retreat because you want to search for the real method to be happy. You do a retreat in order to develop the basic human qualities of affection and loving-kindness.

Another reason is that it gives you time to put into practice the teachings you have received from your guru. It also separates you from the busyness of your normal life, where you are usually caught up in the hallucinations, sense enjoyments, and various obligations you have to others. In retreat you have time to yourself; you are free to think and be quiet, without distractions. In such a retreat situation, you are forced to come face to face with yourself in depth—to meet yourself.

Retreating also helps you draw your consciousness away from hallucination into reality. You can only change your life for the better when you recognize the hallucinations that have been catching the mind and learn to distinguish between what is true and what is false. You become a better Dharma practitioner and a better person.

Without spending time in retreat, the mind is like muddy water. But within a retreat, being alone and without distractions, the mind can become like a calm, crystal-clear lake. There is the clarity you need to help see yourself more clearly, to see your own buddha nature. To realize the ultimate nature of things, their emptiness, you need a deep understanding conjoined with a fully concentrated mind, the union of calm abiding and special insight. There is no other way to be free from samsara. To do that outside of a retreat is almost impossible.

Before the Retreat

Ideally you should do your retreat in a solitary place, which means a place that has both mental and physical solitude. In the *Three Principal Aspects of the Path*, Lama Tsongkhapa advised,

> In this way you realize exactly
> The vital points of the three principal aspects of the path.
> Resort to seeking solitude, generate the power of effort,
> And quickly accomplish your final goal, my child.[93]

Here, "seeking solitude" means striving for both physical and mental solitude, and "effort" means perseverance. You should physically separate yourself from your busy life and, for the duration of the retreat, leave behind your job and your worldly concerns, those negative thoughts of attachment that stop your actions of body, speech, and mind from becoming holy Dharma.

When Lama Tsongkhapa said "my child," he was talking to his direct disciple, Ngawang Drakpa, but he also indirectly meant us ordinary people, advising us that first we must listen to a qualified teacher, one who has an infallible understanding of the three principal aspects of the path, and then, reflecting on them again and again, try to gain a profound understanding ourselves.

More important than physical solitude is mental solitude, keeping the mind away from worldly matters. I think this is vital because all confusion comes from the mind not being in mental solitude. You could live in a completely isolated place but still not be happy. Completely separated from other people, high in a solitary place in the mountains, your mind could still be involved with worldly concerns, with so many problems and so much unhappiness, making a peaceful retreat impossible.

Really, doing a retreat or living our normal life, we all need to isolate our mind from the confusion that attachment and worldly concerns bring. This has nothing to do with whether we are in retreat or not, whether we are Buddhist or not; this is simple psychology.

Pabongka Dechen Nyingpo explained that you should have an extensive, patient mind, determined to perfect your practice even if you must spend your entire life on one meditation, such as on the perfect human rebirth. Having a patient mind, however, does not mean having a lazy mind. You shouldn't think that because you have plenty of time you can take it easy, that you don't have to work at developing your meditation.

Pabongka Rinpoche warned that having an extensive mind for worldly activities and a short mind for Dharma activities is the opposite of how it should be. You should have the conviction that you will succeed in your Dharma practice no matter how difficult it is or how long it takes, even if it takes your entire life. With such a strength of conviction it certainly won't take that long; realizations will come very quickly.

Geshe Kamaba advised us to be honest with ourselves. You can easily think that you are spending years perfecting a lamrim meditation but is that really so? He said,

> We say, "Our contemplations achieve nothing." Why do you think that is? Don't lie: you are distracted in the daytime and fall asleep at night![94]

You might sit long hours in meditation but if you have a distracted mind, there is no hope of gaining any realization. Your appearance as a meditator is a complete hallucination.

The place and duration of the retreat depends on each individual's capability. It is sometimes good to do a long solitary retreat in a physically isolated place and sometimes to do a shorter, more intensive one, or a group retreat. Generally it's excellent to retreat in the holy places such as where the Buddha performed the twelve deeds, in any place of a great holy being, or in an area associated with the deity of your retreat. It is also extremely powerful to do the retreat where your guru is living or has lived. Doing retreat in such holy places is very effective for your mind because you receive blessings of the place. Your mind will be calm and have fewer disturbances and negative thoughts, such as attachment and so forth. It is also easy for you to realize emptiness.

Before you do a retreat, especially a retreat on a tantric deity, there are preliminary practices[95] that you normally do to ensure success. You can read texts such as the *Perfection of Wisdom* sutras, like the *Vajra Cutter Sutra*, or the *Arya Sanghata Sutra* or *Golden Light Sutra*. Reading them brings incredible purification and collects extensive merit.

You eliminate obstacles through purifying negative karmas and downfalls with Vajrasattva recitation; attain the necessary conditions of collecting merit through offering mandalas, doing prostrations, and so forth; and receive the blessing of the guru through the practice of guru yoga, such as the Lama Tsongkhapa Guru Yoga. You can also collect merit by making *tormas*[96] or water charity to the hungry ghosts, or by offering service or making offerings to the sangha. Making *tsatsas*[97] of Mitrukpa[98] is also a very common preliminary.

Retreating away from Negative Emotions

Whatever retreat you do, you must retreat away from the eight worldly dharmas. During that precious time, you need to disengage from the worldly mind, the one attached to this life. Of course, this is what you should be doing all the time, not just in retreat.

Heruka gave some wonderful advice to the great yogi Luipa, one of the lineage lamas of the Heruka Chakrasamvara teachings:

> Give up stretching the legs.
> Give up entering samsara.
> Generate bodhichitta to attain Vajrasattva,
> the Great Victorious One, for all sentient beings.[99]

That does not mean that you can't sleep during retreat, that you are not allowed to lie down and stretch out your legs at night. It means giving up your servitude to the mind controlled by the eight worldly dharmas and overcoming the laziness that is attached to samsaric pleasures. For example, around other people you don't stretch your legs, but if you are alone and you feel a little tired, the thought of getting comfortable might arise and you naturally find yourself stretching your legs. This physical stretching can lead to a mental laziness that might mean you even feel too lazy to do your daily meditation or, if you do meditate, your mind is looking for comfort—mentally "stretching the legs"—causing it to wander away from the object of concentration. The fundamental mistake is allowing your mind to be under the control of the thought of the eight worldly dharmas. In this way you waste a day, a week, a month, a year, until you have wasted your whole life.

For your retreat to be really effective, you need to see that the nature of the whole of samsara is suffering and determine to be free from it. Then you can retreat away from self-cherishing and you can keep your mind in bodhichitta.

Without having abandoned the negative attitudes of anger, attachment, and ignorance, it makes no sense to try to practice anything advanced in a retreat. Abandoning anger and attachment is the very basic practice, the foundation. Unless you do, you cannot hope to complete tantric realizations. You cannot even achieve bodhichitta or any of the lamrim realizations, because those negative emotions are the main obstacles to any spiritual achievements, destroying whatever merits you have and delaying the realizations, thus destroying your own liberation and enlightenment.

It is senseless to do a very high kind of meditation while continuously creating obstacles to realizations by not guarding the mind, not protecting it from those very gross emotional thoughts such as anger. This is something that we all *have* to practice. Even Christians have to practice patience, so I think there is no question for Buddhists.

Therefore, especially during the retreat, these are the fundamental practices: to stop getting angry by practicing patience; to transform the mind into compassion and loving-kindness; to generate renunciation; and, finally, to meditate on emptiness.

You have to understand the meaning of retreat. It's not just about being silent and not eating, not seeing people, and things like that. It's retreating away from those negative emotional thoughts of daily life. That's the fundamental retreat; that's the real retreat. On top of that, there are the lamrim meditations or the deity practice. Doing a retreat like that, it becomes pure.

You must plan every morning to retreat away from ignorance, attachment, and self-cherishing by practicing their opposites: wisdom, renunciation, and bodhichitta—the three principal aspects of the path.

By meditating on *wisdom*, you retreat away from ignorance, the root of samsara. You do this by practicing the mindfulness of dependent arising, looking at everything as a subtle dependent arising, as merely labeled. Or by looking at everything, including I, action, and object— all phenomena that appear as something real from their own side— as hallucinations. However you practice mindfulness, it comes to one conclusion—that everything is empty.

Then you retreat away from attachment, clinging to this life and worldly pleasures, by keeping the mind in *renunciation*, practicing meditations such as the perfect human rebirth and impermanence and death. When you are constantly aware that death can happen at any moment, there is no space in the mind for attachment to arise.

An extremely important retreat is retreating away from the self-cherishing mind. You do that by transforming the mind into *bodhichitta*, by keeping the mind in the thought of benefiting others, the thought of cherishing others.

On the basis of this, if you are doing a tantric retreat, by visualizing yourself as the deity, you retreat away from ordinary concepts and ordinary appearances, the thought that you, the place, and the enjoyments are ordinary. Keeping the mind in pure appearance and pure thought by retreating away from ordinary appearances is the foundation of a tantric retreat.

So knowing what *retreat* means is very important. You should not think it's just about fasting, staying in silence, and hiding the body in a room. While the mind is in retreat, doing those things is also good. Otherwise, with just those things alone, it becomes a prison. That is similar to living in a monastery or living in ordination without renunciation. Clinging to worldly pleasures, there is no enjoyment; the discipline seems like torture, and keeping the vows becomes like a prison in the mind. But when the mind is guarded from attachment, living in the vows becomes so enjoyable.

The mind has been habituated to delusions from beginningless rebirths, so it's not easy. You cannot just achieve your goal by wishing it will happen. If that were so, we would all be enlightened by now. Therefore, in the beginning you will miss out many times, but there will also be times when your practice gets done well. Then, through continuous effort, there will be more and more mindfulness, and it will become easier to remember the meditation techniques quickly and be able to avert the delusions immediately. Otherwise it will be difficult to make progress. You have to put effort into it; transforming the mind doesn't come from outside.

6 : WISDOM

In the *Three Principal Aspects of the Path*,
Lama Tsongkhapa said,

Without the wisdom realizing ultimate reality,
Even though you have generated renunciation and the mind
  of enlightenment
You cannot cut the root cause of circling.
Therefore, attempt the method to realize dependent arising.[100]

Even if our mind is trained in renunciation and bodhichitta, if we
don't have a realization of emptiness we cannot cut the root of samsara.
Therefore we need to actualize this vital realization, the sixth perfection, wisdom: *prajna* in Sanskrit and *sherab* in Tibetan. For that, we
need the subtlest understanding of emptiness, the one of the Prasangika
Madhyamaka school, which shows the connection between the emptiness of inherent existence of both the self and phenomena and subtle
dependent arising.

The subtlest form of dependent arising is arising in dependence on
name and base, where every phenomenon exists relatively, or conventionally, as a mere label of the mind. Because of that, it is empty of
existing inherently. When we understand this level of emptiness, we
are free from the two extremes: eternalism (which sees things as inherently existent, independent of other factors) and nihilism (which sees
things as nonexistent). Only with this middle way can we attain full
enlightenment.

EMPTINESS AND BODHICHITTA

Whether it is more difficult to realize bodhichitta or emptiness depends very much on the individual. If we have studied and meditated deeply on bodhichitta in previous lives, we will probably find it much easier to realize it in this life because of the imprints on our mindstream, whereas perhaps understanding emptiness is quite difficult for us because we did not study it much in previous lives. After realizing bodhichitta, however, the extensive merit we attain through that means that realizing emptiness will then come easily. The best way to fully understand and appreciate the emptiness teachings, such as those of Nagarjuna and Chandrakirti or the various *prajnaparamita* teachings, is to practice bodhichitta.

It is the same the other way around. If we have many imprints from studying and meditating on emptiness in previous lives, we will find it relatively easy to realize emptiness in this life, whereas realizing bodhichitta might prove difficult. Once we have realized emptiness, however, it becomes much easier to develop bodhichitta because we can then fully understand how the self-cherishing mind has us trapped in samsara. When we see how this has ruled our life, we can then see how it also rules the lives of all sentient beings. From that, great compassion spontaneously arises.

Generally, however, I would say that it is more difficult to realize bodhichitta than emptiness, because of the many levels of meditation we must pass through in developing bodhichitta. Realizing emptiness does not require this long process.

However, to realize emptiness we need more than just intelligence. Being excellent in debating is not enough, and knowing all the emptiness texts by heart is not enough—we must also have great merit developed through strong guru devotion and extensive purification practices. This produces great pliancy and gives us the confidence we can gain whatever realization we wish for.

When that happens, a few words can cause us to gain insight into the meaning of emptiness and then attain the realization—even without having studied those extensive scriptures. It is like waking from a sleep; we can suddenly clearly see the object we must negate, this nonexistent object—this real I—that until that moment we have completely believed in.

Once we have recognized the emptiness of one object, it becomes so easy to do it for others, like pressing a button to make an object work immediately. Not like an elevator button in a bad hotel, where we press it and have to wait ages before the elevator arrives. This is instantaneous. Even without going through the analysis of the four vital points, which we will look at later, or using the many other lines of reasoning, just by placing the mind single-pointedly on the I that appears to exist from its own side, we can realize how it is completely empty.

Understanding Emptiness

Emptiness is *shunyata* in Sanskrit and *tongpanyi* in Tibetan. The last syllable of the Tibetan, *nyi*, is very important; it indicates something much more specific than ordinary emptiness. Say we are very poor. No matter how much we want to buy a cappuccino, a chocolate bar, or an ice cream, our purse is empty of money. This is ordinary emptiness—the lack of something, in this case the absence of money.

Although *tongpanyi* is translated as "emptiness," *nyi* means "only"; perhaps we should translate it as "only emptiness" or "emptiness only." *Tongpanyi* does not refer to the absence of the phenomenon itself. We might not be poor, we might have a million dollars in a vault in a bank, but that vault is still empty; the money itself is still empty. It is not empty in the sense of not being there but empty in the sense of *tongpanyi*, this particular emptiness, the emptiness of inherent existence. There is an emptiness of that real, independent money and an emptiness of that real, independent bank. This is completely different from the ordinary emptiness that people talk about. In fact, when we understand emptiness, and when we understand dependent origination, we know that *because* of this particular emptiness, because of emptiness *only*, the money exists in the bank.

There are four main Buddhist philosophical schools: Sautrantika, Vai-bhashika, Chittamatra, and Madhyamaka, and within the Madhyamaka there are two subschools, Svatantrika and Prasangika. This is the correct way of understanding emptiness according to the Prasangika, the subtlest of the schools.

Padmasambhava,[101] Nagarjuna, and Asanga, as well as Lama Tsongkhapa, actualized the Prasangika's view and so were able to give teachings from their experience and guide us, helping us to be free from the oceans of samsaric suffering and bring us to full enlightenment.

For instance, Lama Tsongkhapa used the example of a vase to help us see what doesn't exist without negating what does exist. He said that when we check and see that there is no vase—that the top is not the vase, the neck is not the vase, the belly is not the vase, the bottom is not the vase—if we conclude that there is no vase at all, this view of emptiness does not help us see how the vase *does* exist. Unless our conclusion is an understanding of dependent arising, then we are led into a sense that there is no vase, and that is nihilism.

This is because we have made *the* big mistake and left out the object of refutation. Rather than checking for the inherently existing vase—which does not exist at all and is therefore the object to be refuted—we check for the general vase, and when we see it is not any of its parts we conclude there is no vase at all. This is why identifying the object of refutation is the first of the four vital points of analysis we will look at below, and why Lama Tsongkhapa explained it in great detail in both his *Lamrim Chenmo* and his *Middle Length Lamrim*.

The vital point—the key—when studying emptiness is understanding the object of refutation, the object that appears to us as existing from its own side but which in fact does not exist at all, and therefore needs to be negated or refuted. When we have that key, the lock is open and we can realize emptiness quite easily. It depends on how skillful we are in analytical meditation.

Our understanding of emptiness can only be considered correct if it helps us understand subtle dependent arising and does not contradict it. But if it leads us to the conclusion that there is no dependent arising, there is no object existing in dependence upon other factors, then there is a flaw in our understanding. Dependent arising and emptiness are not two separate phenomena. In Tibetan, dependent arising is *tenching drelwar jungwa. Ten*, "dependent," eliminates nihilism, and *jung*, "arising," eliminates eternalism. That is the middle way: neither nihilism nor eternalism.

Something that arises in dependence on causes is empty of existing from its own side, being merely labeled by the mind, and emptiness is such a thing. In that way, dependent arising and emptiness are unified.

Everything Appears to Us as Inherently Existing

I don't understand emptiness well, so I can only explain it in a simple way. We are nothing more than our body and mind, which Buddhism calls the five aggregates: the form aggregate and the mental aggregates of feeling, discrimination, compositional factors, and consciousness. When we investigate how our sense of I exists, we must see that it depends on these aggregates. The I exists and the action of the I exists because the valid base—the collection of five aggregates—exists. They exist in mere name, not from their own side. Even the valid base exists in mere name. Saying the I exists "in mere name" does not mean that it does not *actually* exist. It exists, but the mode of existing is so unbelievably subtle that, for our hallucinating mind, it is *like* it does not exist. In fact, for our hallucinating mind, what exists—the merely labeled "I"—seems to be nonexistent, whereas we totally believe in what doesn't exist—the real I.

For instance, when we sit—when the form aggregate, the body, sits— we think "I am sitting." Thus, on the action of the body sitting, we merely impute the I is sitting. Whatever action we are doing—eating, standing, sitting, sleeping, lying down—the aggregates are doing the action and the thought of the I doing that is merely imputed or labeled. The sense of I doing that action has been labeled by our mind; therefore, it has come from our mind. There is no inherently existing I, no I other than that which has been merely labeled in this way.

However, the I does not appear back to us as merely labeled but as existing from its own side out there. Then, in the next moment, we believe that appearance. Only the enlightened beings, the buddhas, apprehend it as merely labeled. Even arya bodhisattvas experience this perception of inherent existence when they are not in meditative equipoise directly meditating on emptiness, even though they don't believe that appearance. However, because the negative imprints of the disturbing-thought obscurations have not yet ceased, we ordinary sentient beings have this hallucination of the inherently existing I. This is a *huge* hallucination. For us, it is like that all the time.

First, depending on the base, the mind merely imputes the I. Then, in the second moment, the negative imprint left by past ignorance projects the real I, like a film put into a movie projector is projected onto a screen. The real I has never existed in that way and it will never exist in that way. And then, in the third moment, we believe that this I really exists as it appears. That concept, that this is real, is the root of the suffering of samsara. It is where all the suffering of rebirth comes from, where all the suffering of sickness comes from, where all the suffering of old age comes from, where all the suffering of death comes from—where *all* suffering comes from.

When we consider this belief in the real I, this thing that is the root of all our problems, it is very interesting. This real I is colorless and shapeless, without physical form; it is just a concept, just a mistaken way of thinking. This concept is the total opposite of the reality of how the I exists; it is the total opposite of how the aggregates exist. We have this wrong concept and then we believe in it. This is so subtle, but *this* is where the whole of our suffering comes from.

The Four Vital Points of Analysis

There are many ways of approaching emptiness, many lines of reasoning, but the one used in *Liberation in the Palm of Your Hand* and many other texts is the four-point analysis, also called the four vital points of analysis:[102]

1. Recognizing the object to be refuted.
2. Determining the definite pervasion of what is possible.

3. Determining that the I and the aggregates are not inherently the same.

4. Determining that the I cannot exist separately from the aggregates.

The first point is that we must recognize the object to be refuted, the I that appears to be real from its own side but that does not exist at all. The second point is the definite pervasion, which means looking at all the possible ways that such an inherently existing I should exist, as either one with the aggregates or separate from them. It is called *pervasive* because there are no other possibilities. The third point is that the inherently existent I cannot be one with the aggregates; the real I and the aggregates are not the same thing. The fourth point then shows that this real I cannot exist separately from the aggregates. When we accept these four points, we can neither believe in an inherently existing I and hence fall into eternalism, nor believe nothing exists and hence fall into nihilism.

Even if doing such an analysis does not directly cause a realization of emptiness, it is a vital means of leading us to a correct understanding of what emptiness is. Unless we can clearly see what we believe to exist (the inherently existing I), which is the first point of the four-point analysis, and then see how it cannot exist in any possible way, which are the other three points, we can spend many years in analytical meditation without it ever becoming a meditation on emptiness. We can know that ignorance is the cause of all suffering and that ignorance is believing in an inherently existent I, but have no idea what that inherently existent I is and have no means to definitely refute its existence.

1. Recognizing the Object to Be Refuted

Within the Madhyamaka philosophy there are many ways of analyzing emptiness, but unless we start with this clear understanding of what our ignorance believes in, we will forever miss the point. It is like knowing that there is a thief burgling our house but having no idea what they might look like and so no way of apprehending them. Once we have clearly identified them, however, we can shoot them, drop a bomb on them, hit them with a hammer, or use whatever means we want to free ourselves from them, but we must first be absolutely certain of their identity. If we shoot the wrong person, it will do us no good at all. We need to clearly know both the right target and the means of destroying it.

This is the same when we meditate on emptiness. First, we need to know the object that needs to be refuted, and then we use all the other reasonings to see how that object cannot exist in the way our ignorance believes. Unless this first point is very clear, whatever meditation we do, even if we think it is on emptiness, is missing its mark.

There is an I that exists, the I that is merely imputed on the valid base of the aggregates, but this is not what we are identifying here. In order to pinpoint the cause of all our problems, we need to clearly see the other I, the one that doesn't exist at all, even though our ignorance completely believes in its existence. This is the real I, the inherently existing I, the independent I. It is called the object of refutation or the object of negation, *gakcha* in Tibetan, because it must be refuted or negated for us to be free from samsara.

Perhaps the term *real I* means more to you than *inherently existent I*. All the terms used are philosophical and they may not be immediately clear, but still, whatever term we use, we must have a clear understanding of what this nonexistent object is that we instinctively believe to exist. Only when we can clearly see the thief can we banish them.

Without thinking about this inherently existent I in the correct way, we can never overcome its influence on what we do; it may even make its influence stronger. If we look back on a time when we were in a very emotional state, such as terror from a near accident or excitement from winning a prize or being praised, we will see a very strong, very real I experiencing that emotion. This is the way the I has appeared to us from beginningless rebirths: inherently existent, existing from its own side. Unless we can see the underlying hallucination beneath the strong I that felt the terror or the excitement, none of the various analyses will work.

Normally, when we want to emphatically call attention to ourselves, we point to the chest as if the I is there. The real I is not in the chest; it is not in the legs, not in the toes, not in the head, not in the brain, not in the nose, not in the ears, not in the fingers. The real I is not in the kaka. We are not living in the kaka! If our body were to be x-rayed or cut open in hospital, we could not find it. From the hair down to the toes, this real I cannot be found at all.

If we were to meditate for just one day, analyzing, checking, going to a subtler level, we would see that this real I we believe in totally is not there! However, because we don't check, this labeling process goes on continuously.

Recognizing the object to be refuted must come before we do any other analytical meditation. Just as after waking up from a dream in which we won a million dollars, we recognize the million dollars is a fantasy, we need to recognize the fantasy of the I that we believe to be completely real from its own side. In the dream, we perceive the appearance of the million dollars, then, on waking, we understand that this is a dream and we have the certainty that the money doesn't exist at all. We use the same procedure in coming to understand and realize emptiness. To recognize this nonexistent object that needs to be negated is the beginning of the procedure. We have not realized emptiness but we have deeply understood how this real I doesn't exist.

From the time of our birth—from beginningless rebirths—this hallucination of a real I has always been with us and we have never recognized our error; we have never seen how it is empty of existing in that way. Now, just as a soil's nutrients and water will cause a seed to sprout, because of the nutrients of our accumulated merit and the moisture of our guru devotion, the way the real I falsely appears to us will become apparent. It takes a great deal of merit.

Once we have recognized the false I, it cannot remain; we automatically lose that appearance. It's not that the real I was there and we have somehow banished it, sending it away through the window of the meditation room to go off to New York or Sydney or somewhere far away. It's not like that at all. We hold this sense of a real I in our mind all the time and yet now, at this moment, when we recognize that this real I is totally false, it ceases to be an object of our mind. It was never there in the first place, but now we have recognized it as such.

As soon as we see the object of refutation, we see emptiness. One second we see the false object and believe in it, the next second we see it for what it is and we see the emptiness of that inherent appearance. There is not an atom of inherent existence; there is nothing there from its own side.

For example, we mistakenly see a tiger from afar and we are terrified. But as we get closer we realize it is just a bush. Or what seems like a man when we are far away, we realize it is a scarecrow when we get closer. In the same way, we will see the real I we have believed in for beginningless lives as a hallucination.

Great meditators explain that this sudden understanding of emptiness is very intense. The sense of a real, inherently existing I has been created by our ignorant mind, and we have believed in it for countless lifetimes; and now, right now, this second of this hour of this day of this month, due to having accumulated extensive merit, we see this false I for what it is. Suddenly we exclaim, "Oh! This is it!"

When we see this, we must continue; we can't turn back, no matter how afraid we might be. It's like being in the middle of a fast-running river in a boat; we have to continue on to the other bank. It is said that when bodhisattvas with sharp intelligence see the nonexistence of the I, they realize emptiness, whereas those of lesser intelligence become incredibly afraid, feeling that they are losing their sense of identity. It is very important to understand what is happening and, if there is fear, go through that fear. We shouldn't be afraid of falling into nihilism, into nothingness. When the real I is suddenly not there and there is nothing to hang on to, that is very, very positive.

There is an I that exists. From beginningless rebirths up to now there has always been the continuity of the existence of the aggregates. These aggregates are the valid base for the I that does exist, the one that is merely imputed by the mind depending on those aggregates. This is what we come to understand when we study the subtle dependent arising that is explained by the Prasangika school.

The King of Delusions

I'll give you a few examples. Imagine you've just had a baby and, needing to think of a name for him, you decide to call him George. When you first saw the baby there was no appearance of George. After that, you decided on George. Your mind not only labeled the aggregates of the baby "George" but also *merely* labeled them. If your mind hadn't labeled those aggregates "George," George would not have existed.

Before the baby was conceived, before the aggregates came into existence, that name had no valid base. George did not exist, even though you might have already decided on the name for the baby. Therefore George only came into existence depending on the aggregates and depending on the labeling mind that merely labeled "George" onto those aggregates. So George exists in mere name.

In that first moment, it is just the merely imputed George, but you do not know that, you do not realize that. Then, the next moment, the real George appears from there. A merely labeled George should appear—that is the reality—but that does not happen. What happens in the next moment is that George appears to exist from its own side. To ignorance, it seems that this George never came from the mind, that it is not merely labeled by the mind, and that it has never been labeled by the mind—that it totally exists from its own side. That is totally false.

So in the first moment there is the merely labeled George and then, in the next moment, the negative imprint left by ignorance projects the real George. That is the hallucination. Then, in the third moment, you believe that real appearance. It appears real and you believe it to be real. You believe this is the real George, but there is no real George. There is no real George existing from its own side at all. That never happened. That is the basic problem. It is the king of delusions, the root of all the delusions. All other delusions such as attachment arise on the basis of that wrong object.

To give another example, imagine we are being taken around an empty house we want to rent by the owner, who names each room as we enter it: "This is the bedroom. This is the kitchen. This is the office." Before the name is given, we perceive the appearance of an empty room, but after the owner gives it a name, such as the office, we then perceive the appearance of the office. Later, we move stuff in, such as a desk and a computer—whatever we need to make that room an office. The same with the kitchen, the bathroom, and so forth. First the name is given and then, immediately after that, we perceive the appearance of the office or the kitchen. Being introduced to each room by the owner, we are "taught" the names of the rooms and the rooms appear to us as just that, and we believe in that appearance.

The rooms should appear to us as merely labeled by the mind—which is exactly what happened when the owner named them for us—but this is not what happens. We mistake the label as the reality. Now the big question is this: *Why* don't the rooms appear to us as merely labeled by somebody's mind?

This is what happened when we learned the alphabet. For instance, with the letter *Z*, our teacher drew three lines on the blackboard and told us this was called "zed."[103] Before the teacher explained this, these were just three lines to us; we didn't perceive the appearance of the letter *Z*. Once they introduced us to the name "zed," however, we believed in that. Following what the teacher said, our mind merely imputed *Z* and then, the next moment, we perceived the appearance of the *Z*. This was the label that had been given to those three lines, and that was what we should have seen, but we didn't. The first moment there was that mere label, but the next moment it appeared as a real *Z*, real from its own side, not merely labeled by the mind. Then, in the third moment, we totally believed the hallucination. It appears real; we believe it to be real.

Now, when we look for the real *Z*, where is it? Is it on the top horizontal line? Or the diagonal line? Or is it the bottom horizontal line? Or even all three lines? There is no real *Z* there, even on all three lines. It is exactly the same when we look for the real I. Where is it on the valid base of the aggregates? None of the aggregates separately is the real I, nor are all the aggregates as a whole.

We can use examples such as these to understand how things exist being merely labeled by the mind, depending on the valid base. We can start by seeing how this applies to our sense of self and then expand that by doing a similar analysis on all the other objects of the five senses: form, sound, smell, taste, and tactile objects. Practicing awareness on the objects we observe, we can recognize what is the reality and what is the hallucination.

All delusions are built on the basis of this wrong concept. There is no object of attachment or anger. It does not exist; the mind has projected it; the mind has created it. We have totally made it up ourselves. We have created the suffering ourselves. The real George is a good example of this. On the basis of the totally nonexistent real George there is *so* much attachment. We think, "*My* child." Then when something disturbs that attachment, anger comes, and like that, all the other delusions arise. In that way we live our whole life completely in the hallucination.

There is no real home existing from its own side. There is no real car existing from its own side. There is no real shop, no real shopkeeper, no real money, no real coming and going. There is no real university, no real degree, no real job. Objects don't bring us problems; our belief in their true existence does.

When we see how our deluded mind perceives things deludedly, this has the power to break our belief in true appearances. For instance, the very first lamrim meditation is guru devotion, seeing from our side that our guru—the one we have made a Dharma connection with—is a buddha. Currently, with our level of mind, the guru probably doesn't appear as a buddha but as a normal person. However, by appreciating that we see things through our delusions rather than according to reality, we can understand that because the guru doesn't appear as a buddha to us does not mean they are not a buddha. To other beings who have different levels of mind from ours, the guru appears in different ways, and those who are far more advanced than we are can see them as a buddha. To have the realization of guru devotion, we need to understand this point.

In the same way, we can understand how misreading reality in this way brings all our problems. We currently see a person who has harmed us as an enemy, not realizing this is just an appearance of the mind, that there is no enemy from that person's own side. All appearances of good, bad, pure, impure, and so forth come from our mind; they are all dependent on the mind. Rather than that person being an inherent enemy, it is our mind that determines that they are an enemy. As we develop our mind, subduing it by reducing our delusions, our view of that person will change.

We need to recognize what the hallucination is. By looking at ourselves, our actions, the objects of our actions, and all the things around us—people, places, things, and so forth—we can see that nothing that currently appears to us as concrete, true, and independent exists in that way in the slightest. That way of existing is completely false. What appears as unlabeled by the mind is actually merely labeled.

At this stage, such a teaching might appear very advanced but, like the teachings on karma, this fundamental concept within Buddhism is important to investigate. Although this is not a common topic in Western science—this is the Buddha's science—even scientists discuss how things are not independent. They might not take it as far as investigating subtle dependent arising and ultimate right view, looking more at how things exist depending on the parts, but famous scientists such as the quantum physicists debate about how little independence there is, how things are dependent on the mind observing them.

We should observe objects in this way often, not just during a meditation session. We should do it while we are eating, walking, lying down, enjoying the sun, and so forth. The goal is to constantly practice the awareness of reality, but to do that we need to first recognize what the hallucination is. To know what is real, first we must know what is false, otherwise there is no way to touch on the reality of things.

The View of the Changeable Aggregates

Seeing things as existing inherently, independent of any other factors, is considered the first of the five extreme views[104] and is generally called the "view of the changeable aggregates" or the "view of the transitory collections." It is the root of the delusions from which the other extreme views and the other fundamental delusions arise. It equates to ignorance, but whereas ignorance can be seen as grasping at the inherent existence of both the self and phenomena, the view of the changeable aggregates refers specifically to our sense of self. Like a mother, it spawns many offspring, and we can think of all the 84,000 delusions as its children.

The other translation, the "reifying view of the perishing aggregates," shows us that this constantly changing collection of five aggregates, always coming into existence and dissolving (or "perishing"), is seen as solid and unchanging and hence "reified."

This view that sees the I as solid, permanent, independent, and unitary is placed over the nonsolid, impermanent, dependently arising collection of the form aggregate and the various mental aggregates in the same way a carpet covers a bare floor. And just as we can't see the floor and so think that the carpet is the floor, because we don't have the wisdom to see this deception, we believe the hallucinated I to be the I that actually exists.

The reality is that each of these five aggregates is a collection of things—all the feelings, emotions, and thoughts that we have, or all the aspects of the body—and each is changing at every moment. The collection of aggregates that exists at one moment changes in the second moment, and so the aggregates of the first moment no longer exist. They no longer exist but their continuation is there, moving from one moment to the next to the next.

If there were no continuation, we would only exist for a single moment and then in the next we would be something completely different. If there were no continuation of our mindstream, today's I could not exist because there would be no link with yesterday's I. The karma that we create in this moment could not be continued into the next moment and the next, and therefore we would never have any karma ripening, either positive or negative. If we killed somebody yesterday, we wouldn't have to worry about the karmic consequences of it because the I we are today is totally different from the I we were yesterday. Conversely, we would never be able to develop any wisdom and compassion. This life started with the coming together of sperm and egg, but the second moment of this life would have been impossible if there were not a continuation of the aggregates. We can see this is absurd because karma is ripening every moment, based on the continuation of our aggregates.

Just as the body is changing at every moment, so too is the mind. Nothing can remain static for even a split second. Everything is transforming, changing, moving, growing from one thing into another and dissolving. Thoughts, feelings, emotions, and all aspects of our mind are in constant flux—the same as our body—and that is the basis upon which we label the I. But we don't see the I in this way. To us, the I is not fluid but a single, permanent, independent thing.

This deluded sense of I is the fundamental driving force in samsaric existence. Even tiny worms live with this view of the changeable aggregates. Touch a tortoise on its shell and watch it retreat back inside the shell in fear. If the tortoise had realized emptiness, this would not have happened! For a tortoise, the shell is its defense, something it is safe within—our tortoise shell is the real I, the thing we carry around with us all the time but that doesn't exist.

2. Determining the Definite Pervasion of What Is Possible

Understanding the object of refutation is the first of the four vital points. The second point takes what we see as the real I and investigates how such a real I must exist. There are really only two options. Either the I exists within the aggregates, as part of them or as their entirety, or it exists as separate from them, independent in every way. There is no third alternative.

This is why it is called the definite pervasion; it is this or that, and it can't be anything other. Once we have established this pervasion clearly and we are sure in our mind that there can't be a third alternative, we can then explore what it means for the real I to be one of these two alternatives. These are the last two points of the four-point analysis that show the real, inherently existing I cannot be the same as the aggregates nor can it be separate, thus showing conclusively that it does not exist in any way at all.

3. Determining That the I and the Aggregates Are Not Inherently the Same

If the I were one with the aggregates, various mistakes would arise. The I is the possessor, and the aggregates—this body and mind—are what are possessed. If the I and the aggregates were one, then the possessor and the possessed would have to be the same, which they are clearly not; they have to be different.

The way we see our body and mind as our possessions shows that in one fundamental way we don't see the I and the aggregates as one. We talk about "my body" and "my mind" as if we own them and hence are somehow separate from them. This is similar to how the owner of a company is seen as separate from the company and even from the employees of that company. The employees are not the same as the owner, and the owner is not the same as the employees; they exist separately. The I and the aggregates as possessor and possessed also exist separately.

When we see a table, on the basis of seeing the parts and ascertaining its function, we call it a table. Upon seeing the basis, we give that basis a name. If the table were inherently a table, then labeling it in this way would be pointless, placing the term *table* on the already-existing table. Such a double naming makes no sense. We see the basis of a chair and say "I see a chair," or we see the basis of a book and say "I see a book." And we believe in this.

Seeing the base has to come first. This thing that performs the function of being able to support objects is not the table. This thing that performs the function of being able to be sat on is not the chair. This thing that we read is not the book. The thing that performs a particular function is the *base* to be labeled. We use this thing as a reason to label "table," so it is not the table. In the same way, the thing that functions as a place for us to sit is not a chair and the thing that functions as a thing to read is not a book. They are the bases for the labels, not the things themselves.

Even from this analysis we can see that the label and the base to be labeled—the chair and the base to be labeled "chair" and so forth—are different. This is not the way we normally think, which is that this thing itself we are sitting on is a tangible chair or the thing we are writing at is a tangible table.

Another point is that we talk about the parts of a table. It's clear, even from the language we use, that when we say "the parts of the table," it means the parts are not the table. This leg is not the table, that leg is not the table, the top is not the table, and so forth.

Even the whole group of these parts gathered together—the collection of things—is not the table, a single object. So if none of these parts is the table and even the whole group of the parts is not the table, what is the table? It is the base to be labeled "table."

When we go into a room, we don't see a table, we see the base that serves as a function to hold objects up, and because we have been taught the name, we label it "table." We apply the label after seeing the base.

We can apply the same argument to the real I. If the real I existed, how would it exist? Like the table, we see the base, the aggregates, and we label them "I." The "I" is just a name we give to the ever-changing aggregates. If the real I and the real aggregates were one, however, there would be no reason to label the aggregates that are already I with the name "I." Such double naming is pointless.

Another absurdity of thinking of the I as being one with the aggregates is that because there are many aggregates there must be many I's. We talk about the five aggregates, so that would mean there are five I's. However, within even the mental aggregates there are six principal consciousnesses, so that would mean six I's. Or if we look at the fifty-one mental factors,[105] we then have to posit fifty-one I's. When we break the physical body down, there are many parts—head, arms, legs, and so forth—so there must be many I's.

Every single atom of our body would be an I! Every hair would be an I. When we cut our fingernails, we are killing many I's. When we cut our hair, we are killing thousands of I's. The hairdresser would be a mass murderer!

Imagine if that were so. To travel we would need a passport for each of our I's, which means we would have to carry billions of passports and buy billions of tickets. I wonder if we would need billions of seats on the plane? This is clearly absurd. We cannot ascribe an I to every part of our body and mind, which is what we must do if the I and the aggregates were one.

The next way of investigating is to see that this current association of body and mind we call the five aggregates will have an end. As Nagarjuna said in the *Fundamental Wisdom of the Middle Way*,

> If the self were the aggregates,
> it would have arising and ceasing (as properties).
> If it were different from the aggregates,
> it would not have the characteristics of the aggregates.[106]

Our mind joined the fertilized egg in our mother's womb and it will separate from the body at the time of our death. If this I were one with the aggregates, it would also have to end. That would mean that this I does not have a continuation; it does not reincarnate. There would be no future lives and there could not have been past lives. There would be no way to experience the results of past karma because that I that created it and this I that experiences things now are not the same, each linked to different aggregates. The cause of having a headache or injuring ourselves when we fall down comes from negative actions we did in previous lives. That could not be so if this assertion were true.

Why is there suffering? From the very first moment in our mother's womb, we have been subject to suffering. No suffering occurs without a prior cause. But if the I were one with the aggregates and hence began with the conception in our mother's womb as this set of aggregates did, there would be no prior cause at all and so suffering in that first moment of existence—and all consequent moments, which also require a prior cause—would be impossible.

When we accept that the I is not one with the aggregates, this mistake does not occur. The current association of body and mind will finish but the merely labeled "I" will continue. The I that exists is an I that is constantly changing, that moves from one body to another, life after life, in dependence on the various aggregates, and will continue all the way to enlightenment. That means that the I that is only imputed on the aggregates always exists. There is no cessation.

In his *Middle Length Lamrim*, Lama Tsongkhapa stated ten ways in which mistakes occur when we assert that the I is one with the aggregates. Besides the three we have looked at—that it would be pointless to label something inherently the same; that it would mean because the aspects of the aggregates are many, the I would be many; and because the aggregates arise and cease, the I would have to arise and cease with them—there are others, such as the I would arise and cease not just conventionally but inherently, we could not experience the results of our actions, and so forth.[107]

4. Determining That the I Cannot Exist Separately from the Aggregates

The next point is that not only can the I not be one with the aggregates but also it cannot exist separately from the aggregates. We can clarify this by again taking a table as an example. We have seen that the table does not exist as one with either one or more of its parts or all its parts. Can it exist as separate from its parts? When we see a table as we enter a room, it is absurd to conclude that what we see is not the table, that the table is something separate from the parts we see that constitute the table.

When we don't find the table within the parts or separate from the parts, can we then conclude that there is no table in the room? We might then feel we have discovered the emptiness of the table, but this is not the correct way to meditate on emptiness. According to Lama Tsongkhapa and many other great pandits, to refute the existence of the table in this gross way is not the correct method to ascertain how the table exists. What we have failed to find is not the lack of existence of the table but the lack of existence of the *inherently existing* table. There is a table in the room but there is no *real* table, no table existing from its own side. To decide the table cannot exist because it is unfindable within its parts or separate from them is to miss the vital point.

This is because we have not considered the object to be refuted. The thing we need to see as nonexistent is not the merely imputed table but the inherently existing table.

There is this object with four legs and a top that performs the function of allowing things to be placed on the top. We see it, we merely impute "table," and believe it is a table. We see the merely imputed table and believe we are seeing the inherently existing table. If we bought wood, nails, and so forth and made the base, putting the legs and top together, we would think that we had made an inherently existing table, independent of its causes and condition. If we used it to write on, we would think we were using an inherently existing table, independent of parts and whole. If we broke it up, we would think we had broken up an inherently existing table.

When we really analyze what the table is, we find it is *extremely* subtle. The table is not nonexistent, but it is like it is nonexistent. It is not the concrete thing that we normally think it is. However, because we cannot normally differentiate between the base that functions to hold things and the concept of "table" we have in our head, we see the base and the label as one.

When we search for the real, concrete table within its parts and cannot find it, this real, concrete table we are looking for is the object to be refuted. This is the correct way to meditate on the emptiness of the table. We recognize that the table appears to us to be unlabeled, independent, real from its own side, and then we search to see whether it exists in that way. When we cannot find it and we see that it is empty, at that time we are seeing the emptiness—the ultimate nature or ultimate truth—of the table. As a result of seeing the ultimate truth of the table—that it is completely empty of existing from its own side—we then realize the conventional truth of the table, that the table exists in mere name, being merely imputed by the mind. This is subtle dependent arising.

We Need a Valid Base

We cannot apply any label to any base; it must be a valid, appropriate one. Just as we can't validly label "banana" on the base of a long, orange vegetable (a carrot), we can't label "I" on any random base. But because it is valid does not mean it is correct.

If the mind labeling something were sufficient for that thing to exist, then millions of people who want to become the president of the United States would merely have to give themselves that label and they would be the president, without needing the effort or expense of a lengthy election campaign. If just the mind putting the label on the object were sufficient, then almost everybody would become the king, prime minister, or president, and *everybody* would become a millionaire. To become a millionaire would simply mean labeling ourselves "millionaire." Life would be that simple. Similarly, simply labeling ourselves as an enlightened being would mean we were enlightened, without needing to generate all the realizations on the path or having to purify all our negativities and accumulate all that merit. The moment we think "I'm enlightened," we would be.

For things to exist, it not only depends on the mind imputing the label but also a valid base. Without it, there is nothing for the mind to impute the label onto. When we awaken from a dream of winning a million dollars, of course there is no million dollars there. Nothing in the dream was true. During the dream, however, we believed the dream objects to be true and we had no idea we were dreaming.

In a dream we believe in fantasy objects, but we can also be fooled in waking life, thinking nonexistent things such as inherently existent tables do exist. The lottery ticket in the dream is a fantasy but in waking life we can buy a lottery ticket and win a million dollars. What, then, is the difference?

All things exist depending on the valid base. The dream lottery ticket has no valid base, but the waking-life ticket does. The I buying the ticket exists depending on the valid base of the aggregates; the ticket seller exists depending on their aggregates; the lottery ticket exists on the valid base of the piece of paper covered in numbers and writing. The actions of the I paying the money and the seller receiving the money exist in the same way. Depending on the valid base of that piece of paper we label "lottery ticket," we can win the lottery—if we choose the right numbers, of course.

When we win, we are given all those pieces of paper that are covered in particular letters, numbers, and designs that have been officially recognized as legal money, and the mind labels them as "dollars." When the numbers on those merely labeled pieces of paper add up to a million dollars, we can go to a shop and buy an object that is the valid base to be labeled "car" or "yacht." The pieces of paper are able to function in this way. These things labeled depending on a valid base exist, unlike similar things we see in a dream.

When we investigate in this way, we can see that there is no true, unlabeled independent I, no real I existing from its own side. Similarly, there is no real action of buying a lottery ticket and no real independent, inherently existing lottery ticket, and so forth. All these things that appear to us as existing from their own side are complete hallucinations; they are all completely empty right there. In that way they are exactly like appearances in a dream. However, they exist because they have a valid base that is merely labeled by the mind.

Refuting the Real I

The instinctive belief that this real I exists independently from the aggregates is totally incorrect. If it were true, we would not need a body. We could travel without relying on a car or a plane; we wouldn't need to eat or drink or clothe ourselves; we wouldn't have to work. It would make life so simple.

Of course, that is not so. We have been feeding this real I, caring for it, educating it, working so hard to buy it luxuries. We have found it a partner and had children for it. Our whole life has been dedicated to it, but when we look, we can't find it at all. It's not there. We can only understand this through thorough analysis.

This is similar to the debate that is popular with Western people about reincarnation. Because the existence of past and future lives is not apparent, many people assume there is no such thing, that there is no continuation of the consciousness either before or after this current life. When thoroughly investigated, however, this assumption breaks down because it is based on irrationally equating not being readily observable and not existing—because we cannot see something, it cannot exist. On the other hand, because the mind existed before this life and will continue after it, its existence can be ascertained. Whereas there has never been a person—and certainly no omniscient being—who has irrefutably proved that the mind does not continue after death, there have been numberless beings who have proved it does continue and that there are past and future lives.

Similarly, there is nobody who has realized that things have inherent existence, that things exist from their own side, whereas there have been numberless beings who have realized that things do *not* exist from their own side.

We need to be aware of the interdependent nature of all causative phenomena and how all causative phenomena are completely empty of existing from their own side. When we fully understand the two truths, both conventional and ultimate, we will find no reason at all to follow wrong concepts: the disturbing thoughts such as the three poisons of attachment, anger, and ignorance. Even cherishing ourselves—clinging to the I—no longer makes any sense. We suddenly become aware that following these disturbing thoughts is completely unnecessary in life because in reality the objects of our attachment, anger, and ignorance—the inherently existent objects—do not exist at all. Understanding this, suddenly the old life is stopped and we begin a new life with a new mind, which, rather than being the cause of suffering, is the cause of peace, especially ultimate happiness: full enlightenment.

Of the four Buddhist philosophical schools, the two lower ones, Vaibhashika and Sautrantika, assert that the I that needs to be completely abandoned is the I that is self-sufficient and independent of other things such as the aggregates. This is how the I usually appears to us, as permanent, independent, and unitary. This is the grossest view of the I we can hold and is what is believed in Hinduism. For Hindus, this is the right view, whereas these two schools say this very gross wrong view is the object be refuted.

The Chittamatra or Mind Only school asserts that the real I to be abandoned is the one that exists without depending on the imprints left on the seventh consciousness, the mind basis of all, *alaya vijnana*, from which both subject and object arise.

The Svatantrika school, the first of the two subschools within the Madhyamaka or Middle Way school, asserts that gross self-grasping is holding the I as self-sufficient, whereas subtle self-grasping is grasping the self of phenomena. From their point of view, the root of samsara is grasping at a self that exists from its own side without needing a mind to label it. Such a view is grosser than that of the other subschool, Prasangika. We must see how each of these grosser views of the object of refutation needs to be abandoned if we are to be totally free.

The view of the second subschool, Prasangika, is the subtlest. It asserts that what exists is merely labeled by the mind and therefore the I that appears to be *not* merely labeled by the mind is the root of samsara. That is the ignorance that can only be overcome by directly realizing emptiness, when we will cease all gross defilements, and then with bodhichitta we can overcome even the subtle defilements and attain enlightenment. Until we can realize this we will not be free.

This is why fully investigating these four vital points is so important. First we need to establish the pervasiveness, that the inherently existing I, were it to exist, would have to be either one with the aggregates or separate from them. Then we need to investigate how it must exist if it did exist in this way. Searching for it, it is unfindable both within the aggregates and separate from them. When we have thoroughly investigated, we can firmly conclude that it does not exist at all. This I that is the root of samsara—the cause of all our experiences in the hell realm, the hungry ghost realm, and even the suffering of this life—is completely empty of existing in the way we have believed it to exist since beginningless lifetimes.

SEEING THINGS AS LIKE AN ILLUSION

Everything, even subtle things, should appear merely labeled by the mind, but that doesn't happen for us sentient beings. Whatever we experience is colored by this wrong view of inherent existence. From the object to be refuted according to the lower schools all the way to that asserted by Svatantrika and finally by Prasangika, we need to recognize these different degrees of subtlety of wrong view.

Things do exist, but they exist because they are empty. That is why the I exists; why phenomena exist; why birth, aging, and death exist; why suffering and the cessation of suffering exist. All these exist in mere name. For ordinary people like us, however, everything that is false in life appears true. Whether something exists or is a fantasy, we believe it to be 100 percent true. On the other hand, ultimate reality, which does exist, appears to us as nonexistent.

A verse in the *Vajra Cutter Sutra* says:

> A star, a defective view, the butter lamp flame,
> an illusion, a dew drop, or a water bubble,
> a dream, lightning, a cloud—
> see all causative phenomena like this[108]

Each of these similes is a pointed reminder that we cannot trust the appearance of things.

Like a Star, a Defective View

The first image the Buddha uses is a star in daytime. Because the sun is too bright, even though the star is there, we cannot see it. It is too subtle an object for us to see. In the same way, everything is empty of existing inherently, but we cannot see this because it is much too subtle.

We should also see all conditioned phenomena as like a mirage. In the desert the water we see that is so attractive to us because of our great thirst turns out to be a mirage. This is how appearances trick us. At present we are fooled by that appearance and dismayed when it lets us down. A bodhisattva who has realized emptiness also sees the mirage but would not be fooled by it. Like the bodhisattva, we need to discern reality from fantasy in order to avoid mistakes and suffering.

Things that appear to the uncritical consciousness as real start to seem less so when we analyze them. Nagarjuna, using the mirage analogy, said that the mirage appears to the direct perception from a distance as water, but if it really were water, then the closer we got to it, the more it would appear as water. In fact the opposite happens; the closer we get, the more we can see it is an illusion. The independent, permanent nature of things is the same. Unexamined, things naturally seem to exist this way, but when we explore whether this is so or not, we slowly start to see that the way we have been viewing things is in complete contradiction to how they actually exist.

Our view of reality is distorted. This is the second simile used, the defective view, such as when we have some kind of eye condition like a cataract, we can see things such as fine hairs in front of our eyes that in fact do not exist, or if we have jaundice everything we see can look yellow when in fact it is not. The object of our sight exists but we mistake how it exists because of the disease.

The more we meditate on subjects such as emptiness, the more the false appearance of the object fades. His Holiness the Dalai Lama says that when a person reaches this level of understanding, the way they see the world is not like ours at all. To such a person, the false appearance might still be there, but it is completely transparent, like a dream. This is a highly advanced state.

The route to the direct realization of the absolute nature of phenomena is through what is called *valid inference*. We can't see the reality at this stage, but we can use our logic to understand that it must be like that. There are said to be three levels of seeing objects: as obvious, hidden, and very hidden objects. Obvious objects are things that we see with our direct perception that are unmistaken, such as when we see smoke we know it to be smoke.

The second level, hidden objects, are not objects of our direct perception but we can ascertain them through logic. If that smoke is coming from the chimney of a house, we can deduce that there is a fire in the house, and so from smoke we can use a valid inference to show that there is fire. This is a vital technique used in Buddhism to analyze the nature of things and see the reality below the false surface of what we perceive.

With our own direct valid cognition, we can perceive things such as our possessions. This second level of understanding realizes that the nature of our possessions is that they are empty of inherent existence. We cannot perceive emptiness directly but must realize it by depending on logic, by using the valid inferential mind that sees that whatever we are observing must be empty, that it can only exist by depending on causes and conditions and name and base. This is much more difficult than realizing an object through direct valid cognition, such as seeing a flower with our eyes or hearing a car horn with our ears.

Very hidden objects, such as the subtlest aspects of karma, are beyond even the logical understanding of normal people. For instance, using the fire in the house as an example again, we can't use valid inference to deduce the age of the person living in the house or what they are thinking. It is said that only buddhas can understand this. We must rely on valid sources, specifically the scriptures, for an understanding of these very hidden objects.

Until we have reached a very advanced level, whatever appears to us will appear as a real, concrete, inherently existing thing. Whether we logically know this to be false or not, we will still perceive it as such, and our habituation will almost certainly make us act toward the object as such.

Even at our stage of development, where we are a very long way from directly realizing emptiness, by seeing the world as like a mirage we can stop becoming involved in the false appearances of things and events and stop making mistakes based on that involvement.

Like an Illusion

Another simile used in the *Vajra Cutter Sutra* is an illusion. Here we need to be careful. The Prasangika philosophers tell us that life is *like* an illusion, not that life *is* an illusion. All of the similes used in the verse point to ways we can view our life, but they do not tell us that there is no reality to life, that it is a total fantasy.

Because of our ignorance, we mis-see the object. We see our car and it appears as a real car, a single entity, partless, not created through the coming together of causes and conditions. This is totally wrong. We place this false view of permanence and independence on top of the actual object and we see it like that.

We pull this hallucination over the top of the objects of our world, like a carpet over bare floorboards or a tablecloth over a table. The masters compare the mind to a mirror, with the potential to reflect back reality, but it is covered in the dirt of our delusions and so incapable of reflecting that reality accurately. It is like reality is a beautiful painting that we have left for too long and now it is covered in dirt and the colors are faded and shapes indistinct. Everything we experience is distorted by our misconceptions.

The way an object exists in reality and the way it appears to exist to our deluded mind are complete opposites. One is dependent on causes and conditions, on parts and whole, and on label and base, as well as on being impermanent in nature; the other is a single entity, existing out there without any dependence on the mind or anything else, and it is completely permanent.

From this distortion come all the other distortions that cloud our mind. Unable to distinguish the real from the unreal, we exaggerate the qualities of the object, seeing things as "good" or "bad" or "beautiful" or "ugly," and attachment and aversion arise. From that comes negative emotions and negative actions, giving rise to all our suffering.

The main thing is to think of everything we experience as like an illusion. A skilled magician uses mantras to cause the audience to see hallucinations: lapis lazuli palaces and all kinds of things that are not there at all. The magician has "illusioned" the audience's senses and they believe that illusion. Ignorance is like the magician. We, the audience, are illusioned by our ignorance, the magician. Everything is like an illusion. We are sitting with our friend having tea. That is happening, but our ignorance has illusioned this as inherently real—we are real, our friend is real, the café is real, the tea is real, the cakes are real.

When arhats or arya bodhisattvas are not in meditative equipoise directly perceiving emptiness only—when they are in post-meditation break time—they also have the hallucination of inherently existent appearance, but unlike us, they do not have the belief that the hallucination is real.

It is like looking back after having crossed a hot desert and seeing a mirage—the appearance of water—but knowing it to be false because we have just been there. Or it is like when we are dreaming and we are able to recognize the dream as a dream while it is happening. There might be danger in the dream but we are not afraid because we know, being a dream, it cannot harm us.

A buddha, having ceased not just the gross disturbing-thought obscurations but also the subtle obscurations, the obscurations to knowledge (shedrib), has no projections of the hallucination of inherent existence at all but while they still see what we sentient beings see, they see it as mere existence, as merely labeled by the mind.

How things appear is determined by the level of the perceiver's mind. Just because at present we see everything as real, as concrete, that doesn't mean that others see it in the same way, nor does it mean that we will always see it that way. There are three types of beings: those who see things as inherently existing and believe it; arya beings who, outside of meditative equipoise, see inherent existence but don't believe it; and buddhas. We are in the first group now, but we can move to the second group and then the third.

By realizing emptiness we become part of the second group. Even though, outside of meditative equipoise, there will still be the appearance of inherent existence, we will no longer be fooled by that appearance and, seeing everything as like a dream, there will be no clinging. Then, by completely removing even the subtle obscurations we become part of the third group, enlightened beings who directly see appearance and emptiness simultaneously in both meditative equipoise and post-meditation. Therefore the way things appear changes as we develop our mind.

Phenomena never exist the way we normal people apprehend them. In fact, how they exist and how they appear to us are completely contradictory. This fundamental wrong concept of inherent existence is the foundation for all of life's suffering, never allowing us to transcend our delusions and free ourselves from suffering.

TIME TO STOP THE TYRANNY OF THE REAL I

We have this ignorance, this wrong concept, believing in the real I and the real aggregates, which are, in fact, totally empty, which have never existed in the past, from beginningless rebirths. This false concept brings so many problems, causing us to be forever worried about when this I can be happy—this real I that our ignorance believes in and that has never existed. When can it be happy?

All our life we worry about this, through kindergarten, primary school, high school, and college. We go to university and get a degree so this real I can be happy. We get a job and earn a good salary so this real I can be happy. We marry and have children just for this real I. We feel once we have achieved all these goals, then this real I will be so happy!

Our whole life is spent afraid of something happening to this I, to this *real I*. We totally—100 percent—believe in its reality, and we do everything possible to protect this real I, which is not there. We are filled with apprehension about what will harm us: "This will make me sick. This will kill me. This will hurt me." We take every possible precaution to prevent this real I that doesn't exist from being hurt.

Determined to keep fit, we do hours of exercise every day, by jogging or working out on machines. There is a big industry making new types of machines for our supposedly real I to keep fit on. As soon as a machine has been on the market a few months, a new one comes out and our I has to have it. Each machine makes us do it differently—from lying upside down to putting our head between our legs—and we are forced to buy new ones because the experts in advertisements convince us this new one is better. We have injections to prevent diseases before they happen and take all sorts of vitamins every day. This is all done to protect this I that appears real and that we believe in 100 percent.

Because we believe in this supposedly real I, we get angry when somebody cheats us, lies to us, steals from us, blames us, and so forth. We get angry *for* this real I. We sue that person, bringing a court case against them, spending thousands—even millions!—of dollars all for this real I to harm and defeat its enemy and so be happy. For the real I to be happy we want to put that person into prison. Every day people hurt and even kill others for this real I that does not exist at all, creating all this negative karma for something that is a total hallucination.

Just as a dictator, cheated by this wrong concept of a real I, can start wars and kill millions of people, we are cheated in the same way. Therefore it is vital that we end this tyranny of the real I now. From beginningless rebirths we have been experiencing the sufferings of the hell beings, the hungry ghosts, the animals, the human beings, the gods, the demigods, and the intermediate-state beings. As human beings we have the suffering of rebirth, old age, sickness, and death; the suffering of meeting undesirable objects and not meeting desirable objects. Even if we manage to get what we want, we are still unable to find satisfaction, which is the greatest problem of affluent humans and gods. No matter how many desirable objects we manage to acquire, we can never find satisfaction, but we try and try and try.

This is not the first time we have been like this, with all these sufferings. This has been our experience for countless lifetimes. If we fail to do something now, while we have the opportunity to realize emptiness, we will suffer endlessly in samsara.

All phenomena are empty; they do not exist from their own side, especially I, the body, the aggregates, and the possessions—the objects of our attachment and anger. To remind ourselves of the vital subjects of impermanence, emptiness, and dependent arising, it is very worthwhile to constantly reflect on the meaning of the verse from the *Vajra Cutter Sutra*, seeing everything as like a star, a mirage, or an illusion.

If we can meditate on this every day, even though we might be far from attaining realizations, having a degree of familiarity will help very much, creating so much peace and happiness in our life. Then we will be able to practice the Dharma more and more, and gain more and more freedom for ourselves until we are able to attain a blissful state of peace, liberation from samsara, and then enlightenment.

CONCLUSION: THE BODHISATTVA'S ATTITUDE

I F WE WANT to liberate sentient beings from the oceans of samsaric suffering, we need to be enlightened. For that, we need to attain bodhichitta and have the bodhisattva attitude day and night, always dedicating our life to being used by other sentient beings for their happiness in whatever way is best for them. Even before we attain bodhichitta, if we can have this attitude, working only for the benefit of others, we can become closer and closer to bodhichitta every day.

If we generate the bodhichitta motivation in the morning, for the rest of the day we can hold this thought, trying to live our life with the motivation we generated in the morning. That makes our life really wonderful. It is extremely good to do the elaborate dedications from *A Guide to the Bodhisattva's Way of Life*, either the motivational prayers in chapter 3 or the dedication prayers in chapter 10.

As we recite these verses, we can do tonglen, the practice of taking and giving. For example, all the conditions of the various hells, like the ice mountains or the burning iron house without doors or windows, have to be endured for so many billions, zillions, and trillions of years, until the hell being's karma finishes. With the taking part, we not only take into our heart all those sufferings but also all those suffering places. This is all absorbed into our heart, destroying our self-cherishing. Then, with the giving part of tonglen, we give all our possessions and merit, and even our body, allowing sentient beings to do whatever they want with them. As His Holiness the Dalai Lama says, with that attitude, even if all we do is help others obtain just a small bit of temporal happiness, that is extremely worthwhile.

In *A Guide to the Bodhisattva's Way of Life*, Shantideva said,

May I become protector for those who have no protection,
caravan leader for travelers,
a ship, bridge or ford
for those who seek to reach the other shore,

a lamp for those who seek light,
a bed for the tired,
a slave for those embodied beings
who need slaves.[109]

Here, our wish is to be wish-fulfilling for all the sentient beings, not only all human beings but even all the animals and the sentient beings in the other realms. We make the wish to become a savior for those who need help and a guide for those who are guideless. There are so many sentient beings who are without a guide in the Dharma and even in worldly activities. For those traveling along the road, we become their guide; and for those crossing an ocean or a river, we become their captain, the boat, or the bridge to take them across.

In this way we pray to become whatever sentient beings need to live and attain happiness. We become like the four elements for them. Shantideva said,

Just as earth and the other elements
render service, in multiple ways,
conforming to their desires,
to the numberless living beings that inhabit infinite space,

may I in the same manner, in numberless ways,
serve as sustenance
for this universe of living beings filling the breadth of space,
for as long as they have not reached satisfaction and peace.[110]

We pray to be used by sentient beings like they use the elements—earth, water, fire, and air—for their happiness. For example, the earth is the foundation for making roads, factories, houses, fields to grow crops, and so forth. Just as the earth is used by sentient beings in so many ways for their happiness, we wish to be used.

Similarly, just as fire is used by sentient beings to do so many things such as making food and keeping warm, and water for drinking and washing, we wish to be used by sentient beings for their happiness. The sky is used for air travel but, in fact, without air any movement would be impossible. Like the air is used, we wish to be used by sentient beings for their happiness. Maybe we can become air conditioning! This is an unbelievable prayer.

Here, the bodhisattva attitude is to make our life so meaningful, so beneficial, as a means to be used by other sentient beings, giving them whatever happiness they want. This is the practice of the bodhisattva, making our mind totally the opposite of the mind of self-cherishing. Having a wish such as this diminishes the selfish mind that harms us, the mind that blocks us not only from enlightenment but also achieving liberation from samsara for ourselves and even the happiness of future lives through having a good rebirth. It even harms the happiness of this life.

If we don't have the time to do extensive motivation prayers in the morning or dedication prayers in the evening, we should at least try to do this verse from *A Guide to the Bodhisattva's Way of Life* that His Holiness the Dalai Lama recites when giving the bodhisattva wishing vows.

> For as long as space remains,
> For as long as sentient beings remain,
> Until then may I too remain
> To dispel the miseries of the world.[111]

We determine that this is how we are going to live and enjoy our life every day: by dedicating it for others. Then there is always deep happiness in our heart instead of jealousy, desire, and so many suffering emotions; we're no longer constantly tortured by the ego, the self-cherishing mind.

By experiencing life with the Dharma and following the bodhisattva's way, we live in inner peace and deep joy, enjoying the satisfaction of practicing the Dharma. Our heart is open all the time, day and night; we are able to help ourselves and other sentient beings. All our work gets accomplished; all the delusions, gross and subtle, are ceased; and we complete all the qualities of the realizations and achieve enlightenment. Then we are able to do perfect work for others, liberating them from suffering and delusions, leading them to complete the qualities of realizations and bringing them to enlightenment.

If we live our life in this way, changing our mind into the bodhisattva's attitude, right now, every moment, we have happiness. We live in happiness all the time, without regrets now or in the future, gaining only greater and greater happiness up to enlightenment.

APPENDIX:
ATTITUDES AND ACTIONS TO BE
AVOIDED IN THE PRACTICE OF CHARITY

Taken from Rinpoche's *Wish-fulfilling Golden Sun of the Mahayana Thought Training.*

The texts mention there are various attitudes and actions that should be abandoned and various ones that should be done in the perfection of charity.

THE ATTITUDES TO BE ABANDONED

- We should not have the idea that practicing charity has no result.
- We should not practice it with pride, thinking we are so generous and that others are unable to give as we do.
- We should not have any competitiveness in our giving.
- Whenever we give, we should avoid the wish to receive anything in return for our generosity, such as receiving a good reputation. There should be no thought of mundane reward.
- We should not be discouraged when we are trying to practice charity. Before doing so, we should be happy we are able to practice it; while doing so, we should be calm; and afterward there should be no regret at having practiced it.
- We should not be reluctant to give our things away, realizing that this attitude is only because we are unfamiliar with practicing charity. In previous lifetimes we have been miserly, and that trait is still within us. We need to overcome this and develop the attitude of wanting to give.

- We should not be afraid of becoming poor through offering what we consider to be ours. Thinking we don't have enough to offer anything to others is a block to our generosity. We can remedy this by understanding how in the past, delusion and karma have caused us to be miserly, which has resulted in this poverty. Therefore if we want to have enough in the future, we must overcome our miserliness. Therefore, even if it means having less now, it is very worthwhile.

- We should not be reluctant to give away things we consider extremely beautiful. If we feel such a reluctance, we can see how attachment to a beautiful object is a block to our spiritual development, and that clinging to the pleasure of that object is in fact a form of suffering. In that way we can happily give it away.

- We should not have attachment to the objects we can give away but instead think that it is inevitable we will have to be separated from them anyway—the object will leave us by breaking or such, or we will leave it by dying. With this sense of impermanence we should joyfully offer the object.

- We should not have negative thoughts toward the object of our charity. If we perceive certain faults in the person we are giving something to, we should not tell others this.

- We should not give with partiality but rather have compassion for friend, enemy, and stranger alike. It is possible that because of limited funds we cannot give everything we want to everybody. If we wish to give to, say, two beggars but only have enough money to give to one, we should give to the poorer but explain to the other, pleasantly and with a sweet expression, that giving to the other beggar does not mean we don't care for them. Nor should we only consider giving to the poor and feel that the rich don't deserve or need our charity.

By abandoning these attitudes our practice of charity becomes pure. We should always practice charity by our own hand—being the actual giver of the present—without harming others, by bearing difficulties as they arise, and using sincere words and a gentle manner. Each of these attitudes has its results.

We can also help others practice charity with such attitudes. For instance, when we are with a miserly person who has never contemplated giving to others, we can explain we have something we would like to give and ask if they could find a beggar and bring them to us so we can offer it, or we can ask them to offer it themselves. We can also encourage them to give joyfully, thus planting the seed of generosity. We create much merit in this way.

The Actions to Be Abandoned

- We should not give small amounts or inferior things when we can give more, nor should we justify our miserliness by reminding others of how we have been so generous in the past.
- We should not delay practicing charity until we have accumulated vast possessions and hence would not miss what we gave away at all.
- We should not harm a third party in any way with our giving, such as making an animal carry a burden that is too heavy.
- We should not compel anybody else to create a nonvirtuous action such as killing in order for us to practice charity.
- We should not frighten the recipient of our charity, such as shouting at a beggar we give some money to, accusing them of not working.
- We should not give stolen goods. The texts say with materials taken with force from our parents or servants. Were we to become a king, we should not deprive a family of their child in order to give that child to another family.
- We should not break our precepts in order to practice charity.

The Things Not to Be Given

- We should not give something that will harm somebody. The perfection of charity does not mean that we always have to give everything that anybody wants. There are many things we should refrain from giving because to do so would harm the other being. In *Lamrim Chenmo*, Lama Tsongkhapa lists these. It is worthwhile to study this list. There is also an explanation about how not to give.[112] For instance, say somebody was contemplating suicide and, being unable to find any weapon to use, asks us for a gun or something. Of course it is utterly inappropriate to give them a gun if there is danger they might kill themselves with it. In the same way, poison or anything like that is considered an inappropriate object to give. On the other hand, if somebody with bodhichitta wants poison, a weapon, alcohol, or the like, in order to benefit somebody else, then it is appropriate to give these.

- A member of the sangha should not give away their robes. They are not supposed to physically give away such things, but they can mentally do so.
- Laypeople should not give away a monk's yellow robes.
- We should not give away our parents.
- We should not offer food to those who are fasting or who have taken the vow to not eat in the afternoon, or offer black food such as garlic, onions, or meat to those who have very strict diets, such as Brahmins who keep very clean.
- We should not give statues, holy texts, and so forth to inappropriate people, those who have no sincere desire to know the meaning and do not have devotion, regarding such things as merely material.
- We should not give away our body before we are ready to do so. Whereas it is a wonderful notion to be able to give our body to others, we should not do this before the right time, when we have developed great compassion toward all sentient beings and hence would be happy to give it. Neither should we give our body if it is more beneficial for other sentient beings that our body continues to exist, even though somebody might be begging for it. The texts say that in that case, even a part of the body should not be given. We should not give our body to the wrong object, to those who are evil and will use it to create nonvirtue, or to those possessed by spirits

or who are crazy. It should not be given to be used to kill somebody else. Such uses are breaking the bodhisattva's precepts.

In general, we should give whatever brings the benefit of leading the recipient on the path; whereas if the gift brings some short-term benefit or temporal pleasure but harms in the long-term, we should not give it.

When we have taken the bodhisattva vows and are trying to follow the bodhisattva's path, we should understand the importance of practicing charity and determine to develop our generosity to the greatest degree until we can happily offer our body, all our possessions, and even all our merit to other beings. By understanding the perfection of charity, we should see how destroying our miserliness and developing our generosity is of vital importance.

GLOSSARY

....

aggregates (*skandha*). The psycho-physical constituents that make up a sentient being: form, feeling, discriminative awareness, compositional factors, and consciousness. Beings of the desire and form realms have all five, whereas beings in the formless realm no longer have the aggregate of form.

Amitabha (*Öpame*). One of the five Dhyani Buddhas, red in color, representing the wisdom of analysis and the fully purified aggregate of discrimination.

analytical meditation (*ché gom*). Of the two main types of meditation, this is a meditation where the subject is examined, as opposed to single-pointed concentration or fixed meditation (*jog gom*) where the mind stays fixed on one single object. *See also* single-pointed concentration.

anger. A disturbing thought that exaggerates the negative qualities of an object and wishes to harm it; one of the six root delusions.

arhat (*drachompa*). Literally, "foe destroyer." A person who has destroyed his or her inner enemy, the delusions, and attained liberation from cyclic existence.

arya (*phakpa*). Literally, "noble." One who has realized the wisdom of emptiness.

Asanga, Arya. The fourth-century Indian master who received directly from Maitreya Buddha the extensive, or method, lineage of Shakyamuni Buddha's teachings. Said to have founded the Chittamatra school of Buddhist philosophy. He is one of six great Indian scholars, known as the Six Ornaments. *See also* Chittamatra.

Atisha Dipamkara Shrijnana (982–1054). The renowned Indian master who went to Tibet in 1042 to help in the revival of Buddhism and established the Kadam tradition. His text *Lamp for the Path to Enlightenment* was the first lamrim text.

attachment. A disturbing thought that exaggerates the positive qualities of an object and wishes to possess it; one of the six root delusions.

attachment–scattering thought (*göpa*). A hindrance to meditation, along with sinking thought (*jingwa*), where the mind stays on a meditation object but not the specific one of the session, such as moving to another deity than the one you should be focusing on.

bhumi. Ground, or level, as in the ten bodhisattva levels. *See* ten bhumis.

Bodhgaya. The small town in the state of Bihar in North India where Shakyamuni Buddha became enlightened.

bodhichitta (*jangchup sem*). A principal consciousness that combines the two factors of wishing to free all beings from suffering and wishing to attain enlightenment because of that.

bodhisattva (*jangchup sempa*). One who possesses bodhichitta.

bodhisattva vows. The vows taken when one enters the bodhisattva path.

buddha, a (*sanggye*). A fully enlightened being. One who has totally eliminated (*sang*) all obscurations veiling the mind and has fully developed (*gye*) all good qualities to perfection. *See also* enlightenment, Shakyamuni Buddha.

Buddha, the. The historical Buddha. *See* Shakyamuni Buddha.

Buddhadharma. The teachings of the Buddha. *See also* Dharma.

buddhahood. *See* enlightenment.

calm abiding (*shamatha, shiné*). A state of concentration in which the mind is able to abide steadily, without effort and for as long as desired, on an object of meditation. There are nine levels in its development.

capable being (*lower, middle, or higher*). *See* graduated path of the three capable beings.

Chandrakirti. The sixth-century CE Indian Buddhist philosopher who wrote commentaries on Nagarjuna's philosophy. His best-known work is *A Guide to the Middle Way* (*Madhyamakavatara*).

Chekawa Yeshé Dorjé, Geshe (1101–1175). The Kadampa geshe who was inspired by Geshe Langri Tangpa's *Eight Verses on Mind Training* and later composed the famous thought-transformation text *Seven-Point Mind Training.*

Chen Ngawa Tsultrim Bar, Geshe (1033–1103). Kadampa master and one of Dromtönpa's three main disciples, the other two being Geshe Potowa and Phuchungwa Shönu Gyaltsen.

Chittamatra (sem tsam pa). Literally, the "Mind Only" school of Mahayana philosophy. Roughly synonymous with Yogachara and Vijnanavada, Chittamatra defines the crucial concept of emptiness in terms of either an object's lack of difference from the subject perceiving it, or dependent phenomena's lack of the imaginary nature imputed to them. Tibetan tradition identifies two major types of Chittamatrins: those following scripture (e.g., Asanga) and those following reasoning (e.g., Dharmakirti).

compassion (karuna, nyingjé). The sincere wish that others be free from suffering and its causes. *See also* great compassion.

conventional truth (samvritisatya, kunzop denpa). As opposed to ultimate truth, which is the understanding of the ultimate nature of reality (emptiness), conventional truth is what is true to the valid conventional consciousness. It is also called *concealer truth* or *all-obscuring truth* because, although true on one level, it obscures the ultimate nature. Conventional and ultimate truth form the important subject in Buddhist philosophy called the two truths. *See also* ultimate truth.

cyclic existence (samsara, khorwa). The six realms of conditioned existence, three lower—hell (*naraka*), hungry ghost (*preta*), and animal—and three upper—human, demigod (*asura*), and god (*deva* or *sura*). It is the beginningless, recurring cycle of death and rebirth under the control of karma and delusion and fraught with suffering. It also refers to the contaminated aggregates of a sentient being.

Dalai Lama (b. 1935). Gyalwa Tenzin Gyatso. Revered spiritual leader of the Tibetan people and tireless worker for world peace; winner of the Nobel Peace Prize in 1989; a guru of Lama Zopa Rinpoche.

deity (ishtadevata, yidam). An emanation of the enlightened mind used as the object of meditation in tantric practices.

delusion (*klesha, nyönmong*). An obscuration covering the essentially pure nature of the mind, causing suffering and dissatisfaction; the main delusion is ignorance and all the others come from this. *See also* three poisons; root delusions.

demigod (*asura, lhamayin*). A being in the god realms who enjoys greater comfort and pleasure than human beings but who suffers from jealousy and quarreling.

dependent arising. Also called dependent origination. The way that the self and phenomena exist conventionally as relative and interdependent; they come into existence in dependence upon causes and conditions, their parts and, most subtly, the mind imputing, or labeling, them.

desire realm. One of the three realms of samsara, comprising the hell beings, hungry ghosts, animals, humans, demigods, and the six lower classes of gods or devas; beings in this realm are preoccupied with desire for objects of the six senses.

Dharamsala. A village in northwestern India, in Himachal Pradesh. The residence of His Holiness the Dalai Lama and the Tibetan government in exile.

Dharma (*chö*). The second refuge jewel. Literally, "that which holds or protects (us from suffering)" and hence brings happiness and leads us toward liberation and enlightenment. In Buddhism, absolute Dharma is the realizations attained along the path to liberation and enlightenment, and conventional Dharma is seen as both the teachings of the Buddha and virtuous actions.

disturbing thoughts. See delusion.

disturbing-thought obscurations (*kleshavarana, nyöndrib*). Also known as gross obscurations, these are the less subtle of the two types of obscurations, the ones that block liberation. *See also* obscurations to knowledge.

Drepung Monastery. The largest of the three major Geluk monasteries; founded near Lhasa by one of Lama Tsongkhapa's disciples. Now reestablished in exile in South India.

Dromtönpa (*Dromtöm Gyalwai Jungne*) (1005–1064). Kadampa master and one of Atisha's three main disciples, the other two being Khutön

Tsöndrü Yungdrung and Ngok Lekpé Sherab (collectively known as "the trio Khu, Ngok, and Drom").

eight freedoms. The eight states from which a perfect human rebirth is free: being born as a hell being, hungry ghost, animal, long-life god, or barbarian, or in a dark age when no buddha has descended, holding wrong views, being born with defective mental or physical faculties. *See also* ten richnesses.

eight Mahayana precepts. One-day vows to abandon: killing, stealing, lying, sexual contact, taking intoxicants, sitting on high seats or beds, eating at the wrong time, and singing, dancing and wearing perfumes and jewelry.

eight worldly dharmas. The worldly concerns that generally motivate the actions of ordinary beings: being happy when given gifts and unhappy when not given them; wanting to be happy and not wanting to be unhappy; wanting praise and not wanting criticism; wanting a good reputation and not wanting a bad reputation.

emptiness (*shunyata, tongpanyi*). The absence, or lack, of true existence. Ultimately every phenomenon is empty of existing inherently, or from its own side, or independently.

enlightenment (*bodhi, jangchup*). Full awakening; buddhahood; omniscience. The ultimate goal of a Mahayana Buddhist attained when all limitations have been removed from the mind and your positive potential has been completely and perfectly realized. It is a state characterized by infinite compassion, wisdom, and skill.

eon (*kalpa*). A world period, an inconceivably long period of time. The life span of the universe is divided into four great eons, which are themselves divided into twenty lesser eons.

eternalism. The belief in the inherent existence of things, as opposed to nihilism; one of the two extremes.

five aggregates. *See* aggregates.

five extreme views (*tawa nga*). They are the view of the changeable aggregates, the view of the extremes, the view of holding wrong views as supreme, the view of holding our own moral and religious discipline as supreme, and wrong views.

five lay vows (*panchasila, ge nyen*). The precepts taken by lay Buddhist practitioners for life, to abstain from killing, stealing, lying, sexual misconduct, and taking intoxicants. *See also* pratimoksha vows.

five paths. The paths along which beings progress to liberation and enlightenment: the path of merit, the path of preparation, the path of seeing, the path of meditation, and the path of no more learning.

form realm (*rupadhatu*). The second of samsara's three realms, with seventeen classes of gods.

formless realm (*arupyadhatu*). The highest of samsara's three realms, with four classes of gods involved in formless meditations. The four levels are limitless sky, limitless consciousness, nothingness, and neither-existence-nor-nonexistence (also called tip of samsara).

four means of drawing disciples to the Dharma. The second of two sets of practices of the bodhisattva (the other is the *six perfections*); they are giving, speaking kind words, teaching to the level of the student, and practicing what you teach. *See also* six perfections.

four vital points of analysis. One of the main techniques for meditating on emptiness. They are determining the object to be negated, determining that an inherently existent self must either be identical with the aggregates or separate from them, determining that an inherently existing self cannot be identical with the aggregates, and determining that an inherently existing self cannot be separate from the aggregates.

Geluk. One of the four main traditions of Tibetan Buddhism, it was founded by Lama Tsongkhapa in the early fifteenth century and has been propagated by such illustrious masters as the successive Dalai Lamas and Panchen Lamas.

geshe. Literally, "spiritual friend." The title conferred on those who have completed extensive studies and examinations at Geluk monastic universities. The highest level of geshe is the *lharampa*.

god (*deva*). A being dwelling in a state with much comfort and pleasure in the god realms of the desire, form or formless realms.

graduated path (*lamrim*). A presentation of Shakyamuni Buddha's teachings in a form suitable for the step-by-step training of a disciple.

The lamrim was first formulated by the great Indian teacher Atisha (Dipamkara Shrijnana, 982–1054) when he came to Tibet in 1042. *See also* three principal aspects of the path. *See also* Atisha Dipamkara Shrijnana.

graduated path of the three capable beings. Also known as the three scopes or three levels of practice; the three levels of the lower, middle, and higher capable being, based on the motivations of trying to attain a better future rebirth, liberation, and enlightenment. *See also* higher capable being; middle capable being; lower capable being.

great compassion (mahakaruna, nyingjé chenpo). The compassion that includes not only the wish for all sentient beings to be free from suffering and its causes but also the heartfelt determination to accomplish this on your own. *See also* compassion.

Great Treatise on the Stages of the Path to Enlightenment. See Lamrim Chenmo.

guru (lama). A spiritual guide or teacher. One who shows a disciple the path to liberation and enlightenment. Literally, "heavy"—heavy with knowledge of the Dharma. In tantra, your teacher is seen as inseparable from the meditational deity and the Three Jewels of Refuge.

guru devotion. The sutra or tantra practice of seeing the guru as a buddha, then devoting to him or her with thought and action.

Guru Puja (Lama Chöpa). A special highest yoga tantra guru yoga practice composed by the first Panchen Lama, Losang Chökyi Gyaltsen.

Guru Shakyamuni Buddha. The historical Buddha. Lama Zopa Rinpoche often adds "Guru" to remind us of the inseparability of the guru and the Buddha.

guru yoga. The fundamental tantric practice, whereby your guru is seen as identical with the buddhas, your personal meditational deity, and the essential nature of your own mind.

Heart (of Wisdom) Sutra (prajnaparamita hrdaya). The shortest and most recited of the *Prajnaparamita Sutras,* literally, "perfection of wisdom," the teachings of Shakyamuni Buddha in which the wisdom of emptiness and the path of the bodhisattva are set forth.

heresy (*lokta*). Also called "mistaken wrong views," one of the five afflicted views that are part of the root afflictions. Heresy is a deluded intelligence that rejects the existence of something that exists, such as karma, reincarnation, the Three Jewels, and so forth, and ascribes existence to that which is nonexistent. It is also holding incorrect views about the guru.

Heruka Chakrasamvara. Male meditational deity from the mother tantra class of highest yoga tantra. He is the principal deity connected with the Heruka Vajrasattva practice.

higher capable being. The highest of the three levels of practice or scopes, the higher capable being has the goal of full enlightenment. *See also* graduated path of the three capable beings; lower capable being; middle capable being.

highest yoga tantra (*anuttara yoga tantra*). The fourth and supreme division of tantric practice, sometimes called maha-anuttara yoga tantra. It consists of the generation and completion stages. Through this practice, full enlightenment can be attained within one lifetime.

Hinayana. Literally, "Small, or Lesser, Vehicle." Hinayana practitioners' motivation for following the Dharma path is principally their intense wish for personal liberation from conditioned existence, or samsara. Two types of Hinayana practitioner are identified: hearers and solitary realizers.

hungry ghost (*preta*). The hungry ghost realm is one of the three lower realms of cyclic existence, where the main suffering is hunger and thirst.

ignorance (*avidya, marigpa*). Literally, "not seeing" that which exists, or the way in which things exist. There are basically two kinds: ignorance of karma and ignorance of ultimate truth. The fundamental delusion from which all others spring. The first of the twelve links of dependent origination.

impermanence (*mitakpa*). The gross and subtle levels of the transience of phenomena. The moment things and events come into existence, their disintegration has already begun.

imprint (*bakchak*). The seed, or potential, left on the mind by positive or negative actions of body, speech, and mind.

individual liberation. The liberation achieved by the hearer (*shravaka*) or the solitary realizer (*pratyekabuddha*) within the Hinayana tradition, as compared to enlightenment achieved by a practitioner of the Mahayana tradition.

inherent (or *intrinsic*) *existence.* What phenomena are empty of; the object of negation or refutation. To ignorance, phenomena appear to exist independently, in and of themselves, to exist inherently.

initiation. Transmission received from a tantric master allowing a disciple to engage in the practices of a particular meditational deity. It is also referred to as an empowerment and can be given as a full empowerment (*wang*) or a permission to practice (*jenang*).

intermediate state (*bardo*). The state between death and rebirth.

Kadam. The order of Tibetan Buddhism founded in the eleventh century by Atisha, Dromtönpa, and their followers, the "Kadampa geshes"; the forerunner of the Geluk school, whose members are sometimes called the New Kadampas. *See also* Atisha Dipamkara Shrijnana; Dromtönpa.

Kadampa geshe. A practitioner of Kadam lineage. Kadampa geshes are renowned for their practice of thought transformation.

kaka. Slang for feces.

karma (*lé*) Action; the working of cause and effect, whereby positive (virtuous) actions produce happiness and negative (nonvirtuous) actions produce suffering.

Kopan Monastery. The monastery near Boudhanath in the Kathmandu Valley, Nepal, founded by Lama Yeshe and Lama Zopa Rinpoche.

lama (*guru*). A spiritual guide or teacher. One who shows a disciple the path to liberation and enlightenment.

Lama Atisha. See Atisha Dipamkara Shrijnana.

Lama Tsongkhapa. See Tsongkhapa, Lama Jé Losang Drakpa.

Lama Yeshe. See Yeshe, Lama.

lamrim. The graduated path. A presentation of Shakyamuni Buddha's teachings in a form suitable for the step-by-step training of a disciple.

See also Atisha Dipamkara Shrijnana; three principal aspects of the path.

Lamrim Chenmo (*The Great Treatise on the Stages of the Path to Enlight-enment*). Lama Tsongkhapa's most important work, a commentary on Atisha's *Lamp for the Path to Enlightenment*, the fundamental lamrim text.

Langri Tangpa (1054–1123). Dorjé Sengé. Author of the famous *Eight Verses on Mind Training*.

liberation (*nirvana, moksha*). The state of complete freedom from samsara; the goal of a practitioner seeking his or her own escape from suffering. "Lower nirvana" is used to refer to this state of self-liberation, while "higher nirvana" refers to the supreme attainment of the full enlightenment of buddhahood. Natural nirvana is the fundamentally pure nature of reality, where all things and events are devoid of any inherent, intrinsic, or independent reality.

loving-kindness (*maitri, yiong jampa*). In the context of the seven points of cause and effect, the wish for all beings to have happiness and its causes, with the added dimension of *yiong* ("beautiful" or "affection-ate"); often translated as "affectionate loving-kindness." Rinpoche suggests this is the "loving-kindness of seeing others in beauty."

lower capable being. The first of the three levels of practice or scopes, the lower capable being has the goal of a better future existence. *See also* middle capable being; higher capable being; graduated path of the three capable beings.

lower realms. The three realms of cyclic existence with the most suffering: the hell, hungry ghost, and animal realms.

lung. Literally, "wind." The state in which the winds within the body are unbalanced or blocked, thus causing various illnesses. Can also refer to an oral transmission.

Madhyamaka (*Umapa*). The Middle Way school of Buddhist philoso-phy; a system of analysis founded by Nagarjuna, based on the *Prajna-paramita*, or Perfection of Wisdom, sutras of Shakyamuni Buddha, and considered to be the supreme presentation of the wisdom of emptiness. This view holds that all phenomena are dependent originations and thereby avoids the mistaken extremes of self-existence and nonexistence, or eternalism and nihilism. It has two divisions, Svatantrika and Prasangika. With Chittamatra, one of the two Mahayana schools of philosophy.

Mahayana. Literally, "Great Vehicle." It is one of the two general divisions of Buddhism. Mahayana practitioners' motivation for following the Dharma path is principally their intense wish for all mother sentient beings to be liberated from conditioned existence, or samsara, and to attain the full enlightenment of buddhahood. The Mahayana has two divisions, Paramitayana (Sutrayana) and Vajrayana (a.k.a. Tantrayana or Mantrayana).

Maitreya (Jampa). After Shakyamuni Buddha, the next (fifth) of the thousand buddhas of this fortunate eon to descend to turn the wheel of Dharma. Presently residing in the pure land of Tushita (Ganden). Recipient of the method lineage of Shakyamuni Buddha's teachings, which, in a mystical transmission, he passed on to Asanga.

mandala (khyilkhor). A circular diagram symbolic of the entire universe. The abode of a meditational deity.

mantra. Literally, "mind protection." Mantras are Sanskrit syllables—usually recited in conjunction with the practice of a particular meditational deity—and embody the qualities of the deity with which they are associated.

meditation (gom). Familiarization of the mind with a virtuous object. There are two types: single-pointed, also called stabilizing, placement, or fixed; and analytic or insight meditation. *See also* analytical meditation and single-pointed concentration.

meditative equipoise (samapatti, nyamzhak). A state of single-pointed concentration achieved within a formal meditation session, usually in the context of calm abiding and special insight, which is lost outside the meditation session.

mental factors (chaitasika dharma; semlay jungwa chö). Literally "arising from the mind," a mental factor, as defined by Vasubandhu, is a secondary aspect of the mind that apprehends a particular quality of the object that the main mind is perceiving. There are traditionally fifty-one mental factors divided into six groups: five omnipresent factors, five object-determining factors, eleven virtuous factors, six root afflictions, twenty secondary afflictions, and four changeable factors.

merely labeled. The subtlest meaning of dependent arising; every phenomenon exists relatively, or conventionally, as a mere label, merely imputed by the mind.

merit. Positive imprints left on the mind by virtuous, or Dharma, actions. The principal cause of happiness. The merit of virtue, when coupled with the merit of wisdom, eventually results in buddhahood.

merit field (or *field of accumulation*). The visualized or actual holy beings in relation to whom one accumulates merit by going for refuge, making offerings, and so forth and to whom one prays or makes requests for special purposes.

method. All aspects of the path to enlightenment other than those related to emptiness, principally associated with the development of loving-kindness, compassion, and bodhichitta.

middle capable being. The second of the three levels of practice or scopes, the middle capable being has the goal of liberation from suffering. *See also* lower capable being; higher capable being; graduated path of the three capable beings.

Milarepa (1040–1123). Tibet's great yogi, who achieved enlightenment in his lifetime under the tutelage of his guru, Marpa, who was a contemporary of Atisha. One of the founding fathers of the Kagyü school.

mind (*chitta, sem*). Synonymous with *consciousness* and *sentience.* Defined as that which is "clear and knowing"; a formless entity that has the ability to perceive objects. Mind is divided into six principal consciousnesses and fifty-one mental factors. *See also* principal consciousness; mental factors.

mind training (*lojong*). *See* thought transformation.

Nagarjuna. The great second-century Indian philosopher and tantric adept who propounded the Madhyamaka philosophy of emptiness. He is one of six great Indian scholars, known as the Six Ornaments.

nihilism. The doctrine that nothing exists; that, for example, there is no cause and effect of actions, or no past and future lives; as opposed to *eternalism.*

nonvirtue. Negative karma; that which results in suffering.

object of refutation (*gakcha*). What is conceived by an awareness conceiving true existence; the appearance of inherent existence.

obscurations to knowledge (*jneyavarana, shedrib*). One of the two obscurations, the subtler ones that block enlightenment; also known as subtle obscurations, obscurations to enlightenment, and cognitive obscurations. *See also* disturbing-thought obscurations.

omniscient mind. See enlightenment.

Pabongka Dechen Nyingpo (1871–1941). Pabongka Rinpoche was the root guru of His Holiness the Dalai Lama's senior and junior tutors. He also gave the teachings compiled in *Liberation in the Palm of Your Hand.*

perfect human rebirth. The rare human state, qualified by eight freedoms and ten richnesses, which is the ideal condition for practicing the Dharma and attaining enlightenment. *See also* eight freedoms; ten richnesses.

Perfection of Wisdom (*Prajnaparamita*). Sutras pertaining to the Buddha's second teaching, or turning of the wheel of Dharma, in which the wisdom of emptiness and the path of the bodhisattva were set forth.

perfections (*paramita*). *See* six perfections.

Prasangika Madhyamaka (*Uma thalgyurpa*). The Middle Way Consequence school, a subschool of the Middle Way school of Buddhist philosophy. *See also* Madhyamaka; Svatantrika Madhyamaka.

pratimoksha vows. The various levels of individual liberation vows for lay and ordained, including the five lay vows, the novice vows, and full ordination taken by monks and nuns.

principal consciousness (*vijnana; namshé*). Synonymous with *main mind* or *primary mind* or *consciousness*, one of the two divisions of mind, the other being mental factors; that which is clear and knowing and which perceives its object directly, without any conceptual overlay. There are six main minds, one for each sensory base (eye, ear, and so forth) and the mental main mind, which can be either perceptual or conceptual. *See also* mental factors.

prostrations. Paying respect to the guru-deity with body, speech, and mind; one of the tantric preliminaries.

protector. A worldly or enlightened being who protects Buddhism and its practitioners.

puja. Literally, "offering"; a religious ceremony, usually used to describe an offering ceremony such as the *Offering to the Spiritual Master* (*Guru Puja*).

pure land. A pure land of a buddha is a place where there is no suffering. In some but not all pure lands, after taking birth, the practitioner receives teachings directly from the buddha of that pure land, allowing them to actualize the rest of the path and then become enlightened.

purification. The eradication from the mind of negative imprints left by past nonvirtuous actions, which would otherwise ripen into suffering. The most effective methods of purification employ the four opponent powers, the powers of the object, regret, resolve, and remedy.

realization. A stable, correct understanding of a Dharma subject, such as emptiness, that effects a deep change within the continuum of the person. The effortless experience resulting from study and meditation supported by guru devotion and ripened by purification and merit-building practices.

refuge. The door to the Dharma path. Having taken refuge from the heart, we become an inner being. There are three levels of refuge—Hinayana, Mahayana, and Vajrayana—and two or three causes necessary for taking refuge: fearing the sufferings of samsara in general and lower realms in particular; faith that Buddha, Dharma, and Sangha have the qualities and power to lead us to happiness, liberation, and enlightenment; and (for Mahayana refuge) compassion for all sentient beings.

renunciation. The state of mind of not having the slightest attraction to samsaric pleasures for even a second and having the strong wish for liberation. The first of the three principal aspects of the path to enlightenment. *See also* bodhichitta; emptiness.

rinpoche. Literally, "precious one." Epithet for an incarnate lama, that is, one who has intentionally taken rebirth in a human form to benefit sentient beings on the path to enlightenment.

root delusions. One of the six groups of mental factors, these are the deluded or nonvirtuous minds that subsequently lead to the secondary afflictions. There are six: desire, anger, pride, ignorance, afflicted doubt, and afflicted view. *See also* mental factors.

samadhi. See single-pointed concentration.

samsara (khorwa). Cyclic existence; the six realms of conditioned existence, three lower—hell being (*naraka*), hungry ghost (*preta*), and animal—and three upper—human, demigod (*asura*), and god (*deva* or *sura*). The beginningless, recurring cycle of death and rebirth under the control of karma and delusion, fraught with suffering. Also refers to the contaminated aggregates of a sentient being.

sangha (gendun). Spiritual community; the third of the Three Jewels of Refuge. In Tibetan *gen dun* literally means "intending (*dun*) to virtue (*gen*)." Absolute sangha are those who have directly realized emptiness; relative sangha refers to a group of at least four fully ordained monks or nuns.

scattering thought (towa). A gross inability to concentrate while in a meditation session, where the mind wanders away from the object of meditation. Compare to attachment–scattering thought (*göpa*), where the mind moves to another object of meditation, such as from the deity of the session to another deity. *See also* attachment–scattering thought; sinking thought.

self-cherishing. The self-centered attitude of considering your own happiness to be more important than that of others; the main obstacle to the realization of bodhichitta.

sentient being. Any unenlightened being; any being whose mind is not completely free from gross and subtle ignorance.

Shakyamuni Buddha (563–483 BC). Fourth of the one thousand founding buddhas of this present world age. Born a prince of the Shakya clan in North India, he taught the sutra and tantra paths to liberation and enlightenment; founder of what came to be known as Buddhism. (From *buddha*, "fully awake.")

shamatha. *See* calm abiding.

Shantideva. Eighth-century Indian Buddhist philosopher and bodhisattva who propounded the Madhyamaka Prasangika view. He wrote the quintessential Mahayana text, *A Guide to the Bodhisattva's Way of Life* (*Bodhicharyavatara*).

single-pointed concentration (*samadhi*). A state of deep meditative absorption; single-pointed concentration on the actual nature of things, free from discursive thought and dualistic conceptions.

sinking thought (*jingwa*). Mental dullness or laxity; one of the interferences to attaining calm abiding. *See also* attachment–scattering thought; scattering thought.

six perfections (*paramita*). The practices of a bodhisattva. On the basis of bodhichitta, a bodhisattva practices the six perfections: charity, morality, patience, perseverance, concentration, and wisdom.

six realms. The general way that Buddhism divides the whole of cyclic existence, there being three suffering realms (hell, hungry ghost, and animal) and three fortunate realms (human, demigod, and god).

spirits. Beings not usually visible to ordinary people; can belong to the hungry ghost or god realms; can be beneficent as well as harmful.

stupa. Buddhist reliquary objects ranging in size from huge to a few inches in height and representing the enlightened mind.

sutra. A discourse of the Buddha recognized as a canonical text.

Sutra. One of the three baskets of the Buddha's teachings. *See also* Vinaya.

Sutrayana. The Sutra Vehicle, another name for Bodhisattvayana or Paramitayana; the nontantric path that encompasses both Hinayana practices such as the thirty-seven wings of enlightenment and Mahayana bodhisattva practices such as the six perfections. Because in this vehicle the two accumulations of merit and wisdom, the respective causes of the two bodies of a buddha (the wisdom and form bodies), are gathered, it is also called the causal vehicle.

Svatantrika Madhyamaka (*Uma rangyü*). The Middle Way Autonomous school, a subschool of the Middle Way school of Buddhist philosophy. According to Tibetan scholarly tradition, the school of Madhyamaka philosophy stresses syllogistic (autonomous) reasoning rather than the use of consequential reasoning (*prasanga*) in establishing the nature of dharmas as emptiness. *See also* Madhyamaka; Prasangika Madhyamaka.

taking and giving (*tonglen*). The meditation practice of generating bodhichitta by taking on the suffering of others and giving them our happiness.

tantra. The secret teachings of the Buddha; a scriptural text and the teachings and practices it contains. Also called Vajrayana or Mantrayana.

tantric vows. Vows taken by tantric practitioners.

ten bhumis. Or "ten grounds." The ten stages a bodhisattva progresses through once reaching the path of seeing, the first level being there, the second to seventh during the path of meditation, and the eighth to tenth during the path of no more learning.

ten nonvirtuous actions. Three of body (killing, stealing, and sexual misconduct); four of speech (lying, speaking harshly, slandering, and gossiping); and three of mind (covetousness, ill will, and wrong views). General actions to be avoided so as not to create negative karma.

ten richnesses. Along with the eight freedoms, the defining features of the perfect human rebirth: being born as a human being; in a Dharma country and with perfect mental and physical faculties; not having committed any of the five immediate negativities; having faith in the Buddha's teachings; when a buddha has descended; when the teachings have been revealed; when the complete teachings still exist; when there are still followers of the teachings; and having the necessary conditions to practice the Dharma, such as the kindness of others. *See also* eight freedoms.

ten virtuous actions. The opposite of the ten nonvirtuous actions, and so instead of killing, the first is refraining from killing or saving lives; instead of lying, always speaking the truth, and so forth. *See* ten nonvirtuous actions.

thought transformation (lojong). Also known as *mind training* or *mind transformation.* A powerful approach to the development of bodhichitta, in which the mind is trained to use all situations, both happy and unhappy, as a means to destroy self-cherishing and self-grasping.

three higher trainings. Morality, concentration, and wisdom.

three poisons. Attachment, anger, and ignorance.

three principal aspects of the path. The three main divisions of the lamrim: renunciation, bodhichitta, and the right view (of emptiness).

Three Rare Sublime Ones (Triratna, Könchok Sum). Also called the *Triple Gem* or the *Three Jewels*, these are the objects of Buddhist refuge: the Buddha, Dharma, and Sangha.

tonglen. See taking and giving.

Tsongkhapa, Lama Jé Losang Drakpa (1357–1419). Founder of the Geluk tradition of Tibetan Buddhism and revitalizer of many sutra and tantra lineages and the monastic tradition in Tibet.

Tushita (Ganden). The Joyous Land. The pure land of the thousand buddhas of this eon, where the future buddha, Maitreya, and Lama Tsongkhapa reside.

two bodhichittas. Conventional bodhichitta, wishing to attain enlightenment in order to free all sentient beings from suffering; and ultimate bodhichitta, the realization of emptiness within a bodhisattva's mental continuum.

ultimate bodhichitta (dondam jangchup sem). The nondual transcendental realization of emptiness within a bodhisattva's mental continuum. *See also* two bodhichittas.

ultimate truth (paramarthasatya, döndam denpa). One of the two truths, the other being conventional truth. It is the understanding of the ultimate nature of things and events, emptiness. *See also* conventional truth.

Vajrasattva (*Dorjé Sempa*). Male meditational deity symbolizing the inherent purity of all buddhas. A major tantric purification practice for removing obstacles created by negative karma and the breaking of vows.

Vajrayana. Another name for tantra; the Adamantine Vehicle; the second of the two Mahayana paths. It is also called Tantrayana or Mantrayana. This is the quickest vehicle of Buddhism as it allows certain practitioners to attain enlightenment within a single lifetime.

valid cognition. A mind that apprehends its object validly or correctly. There are two types: *direct valid cognitions*, such as the eye consciousness seeing a flower; and *inferential valid cognitions*, such as inferring fire from seeing smoke.

valid inference. A mind that apprehends its object validly or correctly but through inference rather than direct perception, such as inferring fire from seeing smoke. *See also* valid cognition.

view of the changeable aggregates. One of the five extreme views where we see our constantly changing aggregates as permanent and uncaused. Also called the *reifying view of the perishable aggregates*.

Vinaya. The Buddha's teachings on ethical discipline (morality), monastic conduct and so forth; one of the three baskets. *See also* Sutra.

vipassana (Pali) (*vipashyana*). The principal meditation taught in the Theravada tradition. It is based on the Buddha's teachings on the four foundations of mindfulness. It is sometimes called *mindfulness meditation*. In the Mahayana, the Sanskrit *vipashyana* has a different connotation, where it means investigation of and familiarization with the actual way in which things exist and is used to develop the wisdom of emptiness.

virtue. Positive karma; that which results in happiness.

vows. Precepts taken on the basis of refuge at all levels of Buddhist practice. *Pratimoksha* precepts (vows of individual liberation) are the main vows in the Hinayana tradition and are taken by monks, nuns, and laypeople; they are the basis of all other vows. Bodhisattva and tantric precepts are the main vows in the Mahayana tradition. *See also* Vinaya.

wisdom. Different levels of insight into the nature of reality. There are, for example, the three wisdoms of hearing, contemplation, and meditation. Ultimately, there is the wisdom of realizing emptiness, which frees beings from cyclic existence and eventually brings them to enlightenment. The complete and perfect accumulation of wisdom results in the wisdom body of a buddha.

wrong view. Any mistaken or deluded understanding, as opposed to deluded minds such as the three poisons, that leads to suffering. In Buddhism there are various ways of defining wrong views. The most common one is as the last of the ten nonvirtues, also known as heresy (*lokta*) but it can also be either all five of the afflicted views among the unwholesome mental factors—the view of the transitory aggregates, extreme views, views of superiority of belief, views of superiority of morality and discipline, and mistaken or wrong views—or the last one alone.

Yeshe, Lama (1935–1984). Born and educated in Tibet, he fled to India, where he met his chief disciple, Lama Zopa Rinpoche. They began teaching Westerners at Kopan Monastery in 1969 and founded the Foundation for the Preservation of the Mahayana Tradition (FPMT) in 1975.

yogi. A highly realized male meditator.

NOTES

1. Rinpoche tends to use the term *paramita* rather than *perfection* (which he saves for samsaric perfections). But because this subject is generally known as the six perfections, we have used that term throughout. "Transcendental perfection" is another translation, closer to the Sanskrit, which consists of *param*, or "other side," and *ita*, or "to go."

2. Rinpoche often refers to the historical Buddha as Guru Shakyamuni Buddha, placing "Guru" before his name to remind us of the inseparability of our own guru and the Buddha.

3. Buddhism cites two truths: conventional truth (*samvritisatya, kunzop denpa*) and ultimate truth (*paramarthasatya, döndam denpa*). Rinpoche usually calls conventional truth "all-obscuring truth," "truth for the all-obscuring mind," or "concealer truth," because while on one level it is a truth for a valid conventional consciousness, at a deeper level it obscures the ultimate nature of the object.

4. Tsongkhapa (1357–1419) is the founder of the Geluk tradition of Tibetan Buddhism. Gyaltsap Dharma Rinchen (1364–1462) was born in the Tsang province of central Tibet. He became the first Ganden Tripa (throne holder) of the Geluk tradition after Lama Tsongkhapa's death.

5. A path to liberation or enlightenment that accords with the teachings of the Buddha, specifically the fourth noble truth, the truth of the path that leads to cessation.

6. Although this is often called the perfection of generosity, over the forty years Rinpoche has been teaching on it he has overwhelmingly used the term *charity*, so we will keep to that.

7. See Rinpoche's *Bodhichitta: Practice for a Meaningful Life* (Zopa 2019), 208–16, for more on tonglen.

8. Pabongka Rinpoche (1871–1941) was the root guru of His Holiness the Dalai Lama's senior and junior tutors. He also gave the teachings compiled in *Liberation in the Palm of Your Hand*.

9. Shantideva 5.9–11, as translated by L. O. Gómez, forthcoming.

10. See the appendix for Rinpoche's teaching on attitudes and actions to be avoided.

11. The two kinds of merit are the *merit of virtue*, accumulating merit through the method side of the path, and the *merit of wisdom*, where we develop an understanding of the ultimate nature of reality, such as emptiness.

12. The Kadampa geshe Chekawa Yeshé Dorjé (1101–1175) wrote *Seven-Point Mind Training*, inspired by Geshe Langri Tangpa's *Eight Verses on Mind Training*.

13. The volume of stories, mostly in Pali, that relate the lives of the Buddha before he became enlightened.

14. One of the first of the Foundation for the Preservation of the Mahayana Tradition (FPMT) centers, it operated between 1976 and 1983.

15. The four ways are the kindness of (1) giving us this body, (2) protecting us from life's dangers, (3) leading us on the path of the world, and (4) bearing many hardships for us. See Rinpoche's *Bodhichitta: Practice for a Meaningful Life* (Zopa 2019), 121–35.

16. Kyabje Serkong Rinpoche (1914–1983) was born in Lhokha, southern Tibet, the son of the first Serkong Dorjé Chang and an incarnation of Dharma Dodé. After studying at Ganden Monastery, he became a lharampa geshe, and was one of seven *tsenshap*, or "master debate partners," to His Holiness the Fourteenth Dalai Lama.

17. Rinpoche has covered this topic in many teachings, and there are many references to it in other books. For instance, on how to do this practice, see *Liberating Animals from the Danger of Death* (Zopa 2015) or *Dear Lama Zopa* (Zopa 2013a), 16–20.

18. The *five paths* are the paths upon which a being progresses to liberation and enlightenment. They are the paths of merit, preparation, seeing, meditation, and no more learning.

19. The five great mantras are the mantra of Kunrik, the mantra of Buddha Mitukpa, the Stainless Pinnacle, the Wish-Granting Wheel mantra, and the mantra of Namgyalma. These and the ten great mantras are incredibly beneficial when a being is dying or dead. See *Heart Practices for Death and Dying* (Zopa 2008).

20. After becoming a monk in 1976, Venerable Roger Kunsang has been Rinpoche's full-time attendant since 1986 and member of the FPMT Board of Directors since 1989.

21. Also called the five uninterrupted negative karmas (*panchanantarya, tsam mé nga*), they are so powerful they cause a being to be reborn in the hell realm immediately after death, without any possible intervening other rebirth. They are having killed one's mother, having killed one's father, having killed an arhat, maliciously drawing blood from a buddha, and causing a schism in the sangha.

22. An Indian scholar of the fourth century and brother of Asanga, Vasubandhu wrote many commentaries and philosophical texts, including the *Abhidharmakosha*. He cofounded the Chittamatra school and is one of six great Indian scholars known as the Six Ornaments.

23. The *Treasury of Knowledge* (*Abhidharmakosha*) by Vasubandhu is one of the five great philosophical texts studied in the Geluk monasteries.

24. See also Rinpoche's *The Yoga of Eating Food* (Zopa 2003).

25. Tsongkhapa vv. 25–26, as translated by Jinpa 2007, 3.

26. Shantideva 4.15–17.

27. Shantideva 4.18–19.

28. The *eight freedoms* are freedom from being born (1) as a hell being, (2) as a hungry ghost, (3) as an animal, (4) as a long-life god, (5) in a dark age when no buddha has descended, (6) as a barbarian, (7) as a fool, and (8) as a heretic. The *ten richnesses* are being born (1) as a human being, (2) in a Dharma country, (3) with perfect mental and physical faculties, (4) free from the five immediate negativities, (5) having devotion to the Buddha's teachings, (6) when a buddha has descended, (7) when the teachings have been revealed, (8) when the complete teachings still exist, (9) when there are still followers of the teachings, and (10) having the necessary conditions to practice Dharma, such as the kindness of others. See Rinpoche's *The Perfect Human Rebirth* (Zopa 2013b).

29. The nine levels of concentration are (1) directed attention, (2) continuous attention, (3) resurgent attention, (4) close attention, (5) tamed attention, (6) pacified atten-

tion, (7) fully pacified attention, (8) single-pointed attention, (9) balanced attention, with shamatha as the tenth stage. See Wallace 2006.

30. Nagarjuna v. 7, as translated by the Padmakara Translation Group 2005, 27.

31. Tsongkhapa vol. 2, 2002, 144–50.

32. This refers to the subtle psychic energy that flows through energy channels in the body and allows the body to function. The mind is said to ride on this wind like a rider on a horse.

33. The final nirvana the Buddha attained when he passed away in Kushinagar.

34. From the *Mahaparinibbanasutra* of the *Dighanikaya*, quoted in Rahula 1974, 136.

35. Heresy (*lokta*), also called "mistaken wrong views," in the Buddhist context, refers to the deluded intelligence that rejects the existence of something that exists, such as karma, reincarnation, the Three Jewels, and so forth, and ascribes existence to that which is nonexistent, such as the sense of an inherently existing I. It is also holding incorrect views about the guru.

36. The ten virtues are (1) renouncing killing and protecting the lives of others, (2) renouncing stealing and practicing generosity, (3) renouncing sexual misconduct and being faithful, (4) renouncing lying and telling the truth, (5) renouncing harsh words and speaking gently, (6) renouncing divisive speech and working toward harmony, (7) renouncing idle gossip and speaking meaningfully, (8) renouncing covetousness and rejoicing in the fortune of others, (9) renouncing ill will and wishing well of others, and (10) renouncing heresy and seeking the right view.

37. Step-by-step instructions for how to practice a particular tantric deity.

38. Although the four means are often listed entirely separately from the six perfections, Pabongka Rinpoche in *Liberation in the Palm of Your Hand* explained these come under this morality. See Pabongka 1991, 580, 650, for an explanation of the four means.

39. Geshe Rabten (1920–1986) was a religious assistant to His Holiness the Dalai Lama before moving to Switzerland in 1975.

40. The twelve deeds are (1) descending from Tushita Heaven, (2) entering his mother's womb, (3) birth, (4) studying arts and handicrafts, (5) enjoying life in the palace, (6) renunciation, (7) undertaking ascetic practices, (8) going to Bodhgaya, (9) defeating the negative forces (Mara), (10) attaining enlightenment, (11) turning the wheel of Dharma, and (12) entering parinirvana.

41. See Pabongka 1991, 580–81.

42. The subject of the Buddha's first turning of the wheel of Dharma, the four noble truths are (1) the truth of suffering, (2) the truth of the origin of suffering, (3) the truth of the cessation of suffering, and (4) the truth of the path leading to the cessation of suffering as seen by an arya.

43. The *ten bhumis*, or grounds, are the stages a bodhisattva progresses through once reaching the path of seeing. The first bhumi is there, on the path of seeing; the second through seventh are during the path of meditation; and the eighth to tenth are during the path of no more learning.

44. Shantideva 6.1.

45. Shantideva 6.42–44.

46. Shantideva 6.110.

47. Translated by Thupten Jinpa in Gyaltchok and Gyalsten 2006, 276.

48. Shantideva 5.13–14.
49. See Tsongkhapa 2000, vol. 1, 290–91.
50. See also Rinpoche's upcoming *Patience* (Wisdom Publications, 2020), in which he explores the patience chapter of *A Guide to the Bodhisattva's Way of Life* in depth.
51. Shantideva 6.10.
52. Rinpoche has taught on these thought-transformation practices in books such as *The Door to Satisfaction* (Zopa 1994) and *Transforming Problems into Happiness* (Zopa 2001).
53. Shantideva 6.14.
54. An eleventh-century Kadampa practitioner and follower of Atisha, he was a robber before he renounced his life of crime and was ordained.
55. Shantideva 7.1–2 (part).
56. Atisha Dipamkara Shrijnana (982–1054) was the renowned Indian master who went to Tibet in 1042 to help in the revival of Buddhism and establish the Kadam tradition.
57. Yeshé Gyaltsen 8.18–19, as translated by Jinpa 2008, 555.
58. Shantideva 8.1.
59. Quoted in Rinpoche's *The Door to Satisfaction* (Zopa 1994), 75. *Opening the Door of Dharma: The Initial Stage of Training the Mind in the Graduated Path to Enlightenment* by Lodrö Gyaltsen (1402–1471) is the text upon which *The Door to Satisfaction* is based and is the inspiration for Rinpoche's *How to Practice Dharma* (Zopa 2012b).
60. Shantideva 5.1–3.
61. Nagarjuna v. 117, as translated by the Padmakara Translation Group 2005, 58.
62. *Dhammapada* v. 183. Taken from *Essential Buddhist Prayers*, Vol. 1, 2008 (FPMT), 75–76.
63. Shantideva 5.4–6.
64. His Holiness Zong Rinpoche (1905–1984) was a powerful Geluk lama renowned for his wrathful aspect, who had impeccable knowledge of Tibetan Buddhist rituals, art, and science.
65. Quoted in Sopa 2008, vol. 3, 422. *Compendium of the Perfections* (*paramita samasa nama*) is attributed to Aryashura or Ashvagosha.
66. Quoted in Gampopa 1998, 213, as translated by Khenpo Konchog Gyaltsen Rinpoche.
67. *Guru Puja* v. 105.
68. They are (1) the hell of being alive again and again; (2) the black-line hell; (3) the gathered and crushed hell; (4) the hell of crying; (5) the hell of great crying; (6) the hot hell; (7) the extremely hot hell; and (8) the inexhaustible hot hell, also known as avici hell or vajra hell.
69. Asanga and Maitreya 8.19. This is Rinpoche's translation. Compare with Thurman's in *The Universal Vehicle Discourse Literature*, 2005, 70: "She, the spiritual victor-child, relies on highest striving to bring hosts of beings to a superior maturity; she does not lose heart in ten million eons in order to bring about even a single virtuous thought in one other (being)."
70. Shantideva 7.2 (part).
71. Shantideva 7.3.
72. The eight worldly dharmas or concerns are (1) being happy when given gifts and (2) being unhappy when not given them; (3) wanting to be happy and (4) not wanting

to be unhappy; (5) wanting praise and (6) not wanting criticism; (7) wanting a good reputation and (8) not wanting a bad reputation. See Rinpoche's *How to Practice Dharma* (Zopa 2012b).

73. Shantideva 7.14.

74. Also called "wish-fulfilling jewel," a jewel that brings its possessor everything worldly they desire.

75. Quoted in Pabongka 2006, 311.

76. *Udanavarga* 1.22. This is the common reading. See also the wonderful 1883 translation, which reads "The end of all that has been hoarded is to be spent; / the end of what has been lifted up is to be cast down; / the end of meeting is separation; / the end of life is death." Available online at https://archive.org/details/in.ernet. dli.2015.283948, accessed August 8, 2018.

77. Quoted in Pabongka 1991, 304.

78. Shantideva 7.30.

79. Shantideva 7.39–40.

80. Shantideva 7.46–48.

81. Shantideva 7.68–71.

82. Shantideva 7.66.

83. Atisha 3–5. (The first four lines are numbered 3 and 4 in the book.) Translated by Thupten Jinpa, 2008, 61.

84. Tara (*Drölma*) is a female meditational deity who embodies the enlightened activity of all the buddhas; often referred to as the mother of the buddhas of the past, present, and future.

85. The eight remedies are antidotes to the five faults. (1) Faith, (2) aspiration, (3) effort, and (4) pliancy are the antidotes to laziness; (5) mindfulness is the antidote to forgetfulness; (6) introspection is the antidote to laxity and excitement; (7) application (of an antidote) is the antidote to nonapplication; and (8) equanimity is the antidote to over-application. See Glen Svensson's shamatha chart on http://www.glensvensson. org/uploads/7/5/6/1/7561348/shamatha.pdf, accessed August 9, 2018.

86. For calm abiding the lamrim texts tend to use terms such as *mental quiescence* (*Liberation in the Palm of Your Hand*), *serenity* (*Lamrim Chenmo*), and *shamatha* (*Steps on the Path to Enlightenment*). Unless otherwise specified, *concentration* in this context refers to calm abiding.

87. See Tsongkhapa 2008, 207–8, where he quotes Kamalashila's *Stages of Meditation*.

88. They are the suffering realms of the hell beings, the hungry ghosts, and the animals; and the fortunate realms of the humans, demigods, and gods.

89. They are (1) desire, (2) anger, (3) pride, (4) ignorance, (5) afflicted doubt, and (6) afflicted view.

90. Quoted in Sopa 2016, 27.

91. A buddha field (*buddhaksetra*) is the wisdom of the buddhas manifesting as a pure environment, where they reside and higher bodhisattvas are able to receive teachings.

92. For more advice on doing a retreat, see Rinpoche's *Heart Advice for Retreat* (Zopa 2007), which is where this first section comes from.

93. Taken from *Essential Buddhist Prayers*, Vol. 1, 2011 (FPMT), 145.

94. Quoted in Pabongka 1991, 293.

95. Preliminary practices (*ngöndro*) are practices that prepare the mind for successful

tantric meditation by removing hindrances and accumulating merit. These practices are found in all schools of Tibetan Buddhism and are usually done one hundred thousand times each. The four main practices are recitation of the refuge formula, mandala offerings, prostrations, and Vajrasattva mantra recitation. The Geluk tradition adds five more: guru yoga, water bowl offerings, Damtsik Dorjé purifying meditation, making tsatsas, and the Dorjé Khandro burning offering practice (*jin seg*).

96. An offering cake used in tantric rituals. In Tibet, tormas were usually made of *tsampa*.

97. Small statues or plaques, traditionally made of clay, of sacred images.

98. Mitrukpa (Akshobhya) is one of the five buddha types (Dhyani Buddhas). He is blue in color and represents the wisdom of reality and the fully purified aggregate of consciousness.

99. The way Rinpoche has translated this verse has varied over the years. This version has been taken from his *Bodhisattva Attitude* (Zopa 2012a), 71–72, where there is an extensive explanation of the variations in the footnote.

100. Taken from *Essential Buddhist Prayers*, Vol. 1, 2011 (FPMT), 143.

101. The eighth-century Indian tantric master who played a key role in establishing Buddhism in Tibet; he is revered by all Tibetans but especially followers of the Nyingma tradition, which he founded.

102. See Pabongka 1991, 626–38, and Tsongkhapa 2008, 267–70.

103. A further interesting layer of the concept of inherent existence is Rinpoche pronouncing the letter in the British way. A British English speaker would not even question Rinpoche's explanation of what the letter was named, whereas an American English speaker, thinking it was inherently a "zee," might have to pause to consider why "zee" seems more correct than "zed."

104. The five extreme views (*tawa nga*) are (1) the view of the changeable aggregates, (2) the view of the extremes, (3) the view of holding wrong views as supreme, (4) the view of holding our own moral and religious discipline as supreme, and (5) wrong views.

105. In Buddhist psychology, the mind is classified as having six principal consciousnesses (the five sense perceptions and a direct mental perception) and various accompanying mental factors, usually listed as fifty-one.

106. Nagarjuna 18.1, as translated by Garfield 1995a, 48.

107. The ten absurdities are listed as (1) the pointlessness of labeling an inherent object, (2) the I would be many because the aggregates are many, (3) the I would arise and cease because the aggregates arise and cease, (4) the I arises and ceases not just conventionally but inherently, (5) the memory (of former lives) would be inadmissible, (6) there could be no continuum of memory, (7) the extreme view of asserting ordinary people and buddhas are one, (8) causes could not bring results, (9) we would experience results causelessly, and (10) earlier and later moments on the same continuum are impossible. See Tsongkhapa 2008, 268–69.

108. Taken from *FPMT Retreat Prayer Book* 2019 (FPMT), 231.

109. Shantideva 3.18–19.

110. Shantideva 3.20–21.

111. Shantideva 10.55, as translated by Batchelor, 1987.

112. See Tsongkhapa 2002, vol. 2: 128–38.

BIBLIOGRAPHY

Sutras (Listed by English Title)

Arya Sanghata Sutra (*Arya Sanghatasutradharmaparyaya; Phak pa zung gi dö chö kyi nam drang*). Translated by Damchö Diana Finnegan. 2006. Portland, OR: FPMT. Accessed August 8, 2018. https://shop.fpmt.org/Sanghata-Sutra-English-eBook-PDF_p_2242. html.

Dhammapada. Published as *Dhammapada: The Sayings of Buddha*, 1995. Translated by Thomas Cleary. London: Thorsons.

Flower Garland Sutra (*Avatamsakasutra; Mdo phal po che*). Published as *The Flower Ornament Scripture: A Translation of the Avatamsaka Sutra*, 1984, 1986, 1987, 1989, 1993. Translated by Thomas Cleary. Boston: Shambhala Publications.

Heart of Wisdom Sutra (*Prajnaparamitahrdayasutra; Shes rab kyi pha rol tu phyin pa' i snying po'i mdo*). N.d. Portland, OR: FPMT. Accessed July 31, 2018. https://fpmt.org/education/teachings/sutras/heart-sutra.

Sutra of Golden Light. The King of the Glorious Sutras Called the Exalted Supreme Golden Light (*Arya Suvarnaprabhasottamasutrendrarajanamahayanasutra, Phakpa ser ö dampa dodé wangpö gyalpo shéjawa thekpa chenpö do*). 2010. Portland, OR: FPMT. Accessed August 24, 2018. https://shop.fpmt.org/The-King-of-Glorious-Sutras-called-the-Exalted-Sublime-Golden-Light-eBook-PDF_p_2348.html.

Udanavarga: A Collection of Verses from the Buddhist Canon. Translated by Bkah-hgyur. 1883. London: Trübner. Accessed August 24, 2018. https://archive.org/details/in.ernet. dli.2015.283948; also https://archive.org/stream/in.ernet.dli.2015.283948/2015.283948. Udanavarga-From_djvu.txt.

Indian and Tibetan Works

Asanga. 2016. *Bodhisattva Levels* (*Bodhisattvabhumi*). Published as *The Bodhisattva Path to Unsurpassed Enlightenment*. Translated by Artemus B. Engel. Boulder, CO: Snow Lion Publications.

Asanga and Maitreya. 1992. *Ornament of Clear Realization* (*Abhisamayalankara, Ngön par tok pä gyen*). Published as *Abhisamayalankara Prajnaparamita Upadesa Sastra: The Work of Bodhisattva Maitreya*. Edited by Theodore Stcherbatsky and Eugene Obermiller. New Delhi: Sri Satguru.

———. 2000. *The Sublime Continuum* (*Mahayana-uttaratantra Shastra, Tek pa chen-po gyü lama ten-chö*). Published as *Buddha Nature: The Mahayana-Uttaratantra Shastra with Commentary*. Jamgon Kongtrul Lodro Thaye and Khenpo Tsultrim Gyamtso. Translated by Rosemarie Fuchs. Ithaca, NY: Snow Lion Publications.

————. 2005. *The Adornment of the Mahayana Sutras* (*Mahayanasutralankara, Mdo sde rgyan*). Published as *The Universal Vehicle Discourse Literature*. Translated by Lozang Jamspal, Robert Thurman, and American Institute of Buddhist Studies. New York: American Institute of Buddhist Studies.

Atisha. 2008. *Bodhisattva's Jewel Garland*. In *The Book of Kadam*, translated by Thupten Jinpa, 61–64. Boston: Wisdom Publications.

Chekawa Yeshé Dorjé. 2006. *Seven-Point Mind Training* (*Blo sbyong don bdun ma*). In *Mind Training: The Great Collection*, translated by Thupten Jinpa, 83–85. Boston: Wisdom Publications.

Chökyi Gyaltsen, Panchen Losang, and Jamphäl Lhundrub. 2011. *Guru Puja* (*Lama Chöpa Jorchö*). Compiled and edited by Lama Zopa Rinpoche. Portland, OR: FPMT.

Dharmarakshita. 2006. *The Wheel of Sharp Weapons* (*Blo sbyong mtshon cha 'khor lo*). In *Mind Training: The Great Collection*, translated by Thupten Jinpa, 133–53. Boston: Wisdom Publications.

Gampopa. 1998. *The Jewel Ornament of Liberation: The Wish-Fulfilling Gem of Noble Teachings*. Translated by Khenpo Konchog Gyaltsen Rinpoche. Boston: Snow Lion Publications.

Gyaltchok, Shonu, and Konchok Gyaltsen, comps. 2006. *Mind Training: The Great Collection* (Theg pa chen po blo sbyong brgya rtsa). Translated and edited by Thupten Jinpa. Boston: Wisdom Publications.

Nagarjuna. 1995a. *The Fundamental Wisdom of the Middle Way* (*Mulamadhyamakakarika, Dbu ma rtsa ba'i tshig le'ur byas pa shes rab ces byaba*). Published as *The Fundamental Wisdom of the Middle Way: Nagarjuna's Mulamadhyamakakarika*. Translated by Jay L. Garfield. New York: Oxford University Press.

————. 1995b, 2005. *Friendly Letter* (*Suhrllekha, Bshes pa'i spring yig*). With a commentary by Kangyur Rinpoche. Translated by Padmakara Translation Group. Ithaca, NY: Snow Lion Publications. Also published as *Nagarjuna's Letter*. 1979. Translated by Geshe Lobsang Tharchin and Artemus B. Engle. Dharamsala, India: Library of Tibetan Works and Archives.

Pabongka Dechen Nyingpo Rinpoche. 1991. *Liberation in the Palm of Your Hand* (*Rnam grol lag bcangs*). Translated by Michael Richards. Boston: Wisdom Publications. Also published in three parts as: *Liberation in Our Hands: Part One—The Preliminaries*, 1990; *Liberation in Our Hands: Part Two—The Fundamentals*, 1994; *Liberation in Our Hands: Part Three—The Ultimate Goals*, 2001. Translated by Geshe Lobsang Tharchin and Artemus B. Engle. Howell, NJ: Mahayana Sutra and Tantra Press.

————. *Heart Spoon*. 2009. Published as *Heart Spoon: Encouragement Through Recollecting Impermanence*. Portland, OR: FPMT. Accessed August 24, 2018. https://shop.fpmt.org/Heart-Spoon-Encouragement-Through-Recollecting-Impermanence-PDF_p_1073.htm.

Shantideva. Forthcoming. *A Guide to the Bodhisattva's Way of Life* (*Bodhisattvacaryavatara, Jang chub sem pa chö pa la jug pa*). Translated by L. O. Gómez. Boston: Wisdom Publications.

————. 1987. *A Guide to the Bodhisattva's Way of Life* (*Bodhisattvacaryavatara, Jang chub sem pa chö pa la jug pa*). Translated by Stephen Batchelor. Dharamsala, India: Library of Tibetan Works and Archive.

Tangpa, Langri. 2000. *Eight Verses on Mind Training* (*Blo sbyong tshigs rkang brgyad ma*). Published as *Transforming the Mind: Eight Verses on Generating Compassion and Transforming Your Life*. By His Holiness the Dalai Lama. New York: Thorsons.

Tsongkhapa, Jé. 2000, 2002, 2004a. *The Great Treatise on the Path to Enlightenment* (*Lamrim Chenmo*) 3 vols. Translated by the Lamrim Chenmo Translation Committee. Ithaca, NY: Snow Lion Publications.

———. 2004b, 2007. *Hymns of Experience of the Steps on the Path* (*Lam rim nyams mgur*). Published as *Songs of Spiritual Experience: Condensed Points of the Stages of the Path*. Translated by Geshe Thubten Jinpa. Accessed August 24, 2018. http://www.tibetan-classics.org/html-assets/Songs%20of%20Experience.pdf.

———. 2008. *Middle Length Lamrim* (*Lamrim Dringba*). Translated by Philip Quarcoo. Portland, OR: FPMT. Accessed August 24, 2018. https://shop.fpmt.org/Basic-Program-Online-Stages-of-the-Path--Middle-Length-Lamrim_p_1584.html.

Vasubandhu. 1991. *Treasury of Knowledge* (*Abhidharmakoshabhashya, Chö ngön dzö kyi tshig leur cha pa*). Translated by Louis de La Vallée Poussin and Leo M. Pruden. Berkeley, CA: Asian Humanities Press.

Yeshé Gyaltsen. 2008. *Heart Instructions of The Book of Kadam*. In *The Book of Kadam*, translated by Thupten Jinpa, 529–558. Boston: Wisdom Publications.

English-Language Texts

Dhargyey, Geshe Ngawang. 1974, 1985. *Tibetan Tradition of Mental Development*. Dharamsala, India: Library of Tibetan Works and Archives.

FPMT (Foundation for the Preservation of the Mahayana Tradition). 2006, 2008, 2011. *Essential Buddhist Prayers: An FPMT Prayer Book, Volume 1, Basic Prayers and Practices*. Portland, OR: FPMT.

———. 2019. *FPMT Retreat Prayer Book*. Portland, OR: FPMT.

Rahula, Walpola. 1959, 1974. *What the Buddha Taught*. Oxford: Oneworld Publications.

Sopa, Geshe Lhundub. 2004, 2005, 2008, 2016, 2017. *Steps on the Path to Enlightenment*. 5 vols. Boston: Wisdom Publications.

Wallace, B. Allan. 2006. *The Attention Revolution: Unlocking the Power of the Focused Mind*. Boston: Wisdom Publications.

Zopa, Lama Thubten. 1973. *Wish-Fulfilling Golden Sun of the Mahayana Thought Training*. Boston: Lama Yeshe Wisdom Archive. Accessed August 1, 2018. https://www.lamayeshe.com/article/wish-fulfilling-golden-sun-mahayana-thought-training. For the original edition see also https://fpmt.org/wp-content/uploads/education/teachings/texts/prayers-practices/wishfulfilling_golden_sun_c5.pdf. Accessed August 1, 2018.

———. 1994. *The Door to Satisfaction*. Boston: Wisdom Publications.

———. 2001. *Transforming Problems into Happiness*. Boston: Wisdom Publications.

———. 2003. *The Yoga of Eating Food*. Boston: Lama Yeshe Wisdom Archive.

———. 2004, 2007. *Heart Advice for Retreat*. Portland, OR: FPMT.

———. 2008. *Heart Practices for Death and Dying*. Portland, OR: FPMT.

———. 2010. *Kadampa Teachings*. Boston: Lama Yeshe Wisdom Archive.

———. 2012a. *Bodhisattva Attitude*. Boston: Lama Yeshe Wisdom Archive.

————. 2012b. *How to Practice Dharma.* Boston: Lama Yeshe Wisdom Archive.

————. 2013a. *Dear Lama Zopa.* Boston: Wisdom Publications.

————. 2013b. *The Perfect Human Rebirth.* Boston: Lama Yeshe Wisdom Archive.

————. 2015. *Liberating Animals from the Danger of Death.* Portland, OR: FPMT. Accessed August 24, 2018. Available at https://shop.fpmt.org/Liberating-Animals-eBook-PDF_p_2334.html.

————. 2019. *Bodhichitta: Practice for a Meaningful Life.* Boston: Wisdom Publications.

INDEX

ABOUT THE AUTHOR

LAMA ZOPA RINPOCHE is one of the most internationally renowned masters of Tibetan Buddhism, working and teaching ceaselessly on almost every continent.

He is the spiritual director and cofounder of the Foundation for the Preservation of the Mahayana Tradition (FPMT), an international network of Buddhist projects, including monasteries in six countries and meditation centers in over thirty; health and nutrition clinics, and clinics specializing in the treatment of leprosy and polio; as well as hospices, schools, publishing activities, and prison outreach projects worldwide.

Lama Zopa Rinpoche is the author of numerous books, including *Bodhichitta, The Four Noble Truths, Transforming Problems into Happiness, How to Enjoy Death, Ultimate Healing, The Door to Satisfaction, How to Be Happy, Wholesome Fear, Wisdom Energy,* and *Dear Lama Zopa,* all from Wisdom Publications.

ABOUT THE EDITOR

GORDON MCDOUGALL was director of Cham Tse Ling, the FPMT's Hong Kong center, for two years in the 1980s and worked for Jamyang Buddhist Centre in London from 2000 to 2007. He helped develop the Foundation of Buddhist Thought study program and administered it for seven years. Since 2008 he has been editing Lama Zopa Rinpoche's teachings for Lama Yeshe Wisdom Archive and Wisdom Publications.

WHAT TO READ NEXT
FROM WISDOM PUBLICATIONS

....

Bodhichitta
Practice for a Meaningful Life
Lama Zopa Rinpoche

An accessible, inspiring book on one of the most important topics in Tibetan Buddhism—bodhichitta, or compassion—written by one of its renowned masters who has an international following of thousands.

The Four Noble Truths
A Guide to Everyday Life
Lama Zopa Rinpoche

The Four Noble Truths begins with an excellent elucidation of the nature of the mind and its role in creating the happiness we all seek. Lama Zopa Rinpoche then turns to an in-depth analysis of the four truths: suffering, the cause of suffering, cessation of suffering, and the path to cessation of suffering.

How to Enjoy Death
Preparing to Meet Life's Final Challenge without Fear
Lama Zopa Rinpoche

"When suddenly one day one of your loved ones dies and you don't know what to do to help, you'll feel so confused, so lost. . . . By providing the right support, the right environment, you can help your loved one die peacefully, with virtuous thoughts, and thus have a good rebirth."
—Lama Zopa Rinpoche

Wisdom Energy
Basic Buddhist Teachings
Lama Thubten Yeshe and Lama Zopa Rinpoche

"This is a superb book that presents basic Buddhist teachings with great lucidity and clarity."—*Resource Magazine*

How to Be Happy
Lama Zopa Rinpoche

"Rinpoche works with determination and great sincerity in the service of Buddha's teachings and sentient beings."
—His Holiness the Dalai Lama

Transforming Problems into Happiness
Lama Zopa Rinpoche

"A masterfully brief statement of Buddhist teachings on the nature of humanity and human suffering. . . . This book should be read as the words of a wise, loving parent."—*Utne Reader*

Wholesome Fear
Transforming Your Anxiety About Impermanence and Death
Lama Zopa Rinpoche and Kathleen McDonald

"A wonderful and welcome book for the spiritual well-being of all who read it."—Gelek Rimpoche, author of *Good Life, Good Death*

Ultimate Healing
The Power of Compassion
Lama Zopa Rinpoche

"This truly is an awesome book."—Lillian Too

Door to Satisfaction
The Heart Advice of a Tibetan Buddhist Master
Lama Zopa Rinpoche

"A wise and inspiring teacher."—*Utne Reader*

Dear Lama Zopa
Radical Solutions for Transforming Problems into Happiness
Lama Zopa Rinpoche

"An absolute jewel of a book, packed with unbelievably precious advice."—*Mandala*

Patience
A Guide to Shantideva's Sixth Chapter
Lama Zopa Rinpoche

"Lama Zopa Rinpoche shows us in great detail how to cultivate actual patience, the practice of the bodhisattva: wholeheartedly welcoming the problems."—Ven. Robina Courtin

The Power of Mantra
Vital Practices for Transformation
Lama Zopa Rinpoche

Lama Zopa Rinpoche guides us through the most popular mantras in Tibetan Buddhism: Shakyamuni Buddha, Chenrezig, Manjushri, Tara, Medicine Buddha, Vajrasattva, and more.

About Wisdom Publications

Wisdom Publications is the leading publisher of classic and contemporary Buddhist books and practical works on mindfulness. To learn more about us or to explore our other books, please visit our website at wisdomexperience.org or contact us at the address below.

Wisdom Publications
199 Elm Street
Somerville, MA 02144 USA

We are a 501(c)(3) organization, and donations in support of our mission are tax deductible.

Wisdom Publications is affiliated with the Foundation for the Preservation of the Mahayana Tradition (FPMT).